W9-AGB-795

BLACK PROFESSIONALS' PERCEPTIONS OF INSTITUTIONAL RACISM
In Health and Welfare Organizations

BLACK PROFESSIONALS' PERCEPTIONS OF INSTITUTIONAL RACISM
in Health and Welfare Organizations

by
CHARLES L. SANDERS

R. E. BURDICK, Inc., Publishers
Fair Lawn, New Jersey 07410

FEDERAL CITY
COLLEGE

JUN 30 1977

MEDIA CENTER

HV
91
.S25
1973
c.3

International Standard Book Number: 0-913638-02-1
Library of Congress Catalogue Card Number: 73-80004

Original text published by
University Microfilms, 300 North Zeeb Road,
Ann Arbor, Michigan 48106
Copyright © 1972 by Charles L. Sanders.

Revised edition published by
R. E. Burdick, Inc., 12-01 12th Street,
Fair Lawn, New Jersey 07410.
Copyright © 1973 by Charles L. Sanders.

Revised edition published simultaneously in Canada by
Book Center, Inc., 1140 Beaulac Street,
St.-Laurent 382, Quebec.

Printed in the United States of America.

CONTENTS

FIGURES

TABLES

Acknowledgements

THE PREPARATION OF THIS STUDY engaged a wide spectrum of people. From the beginning, there were always those who were willing to exchange ideas, and provide feedback around my clouded thinking. Realizing how much any task involves many unseen participants, I will take the risk of omitting some by selecting a few whose support was immeasurable to me during the course of this study.

First, I am most grateful to Dr. Helen Hilling, whose interest, assistance, foresight, and encouragement allowed me to pursue full-time graduate study. Without her advice and guidance, I perhaps would have continued to flounder in the professional world.

Second, I am most grateful to my friends, Bessie Wright, M. Elizabeth Carnegie, and Dan Leahy who continuously supported my efforts both psychologically and intellectually. The completion of this task could not have been accomplished without the capable typing assistance of Barbara Jackson and Oliver Burkeson.

Finally, I am most grateful to Professor Allan Kravitz whose shared interest and penetrating criticism provided me with enriching direction in completing this study.

New York, N.Y.   Charles L. Sanders
March 1973.

9

1 | Institutional Racism: New Concept, Old Problem

THE PROBLEM OF INSTITUTIONAL RACISM among our public and large-scale organizations has only recently become a topic of open discussion. The term is new, but the conditions have existed for some time. Among the first authors to speak about the subject were Carmichael and Hamilton, who differentiated between individual and institutional racism:

> Racism refers to the predication of decisions and policies on considerations of race for the purpose of subtaining control over that group ... Racism is both overt and covert. It takes two closely related forms: individual whites acting against individual Blacks, and acts by the total white community against the Black community. We call these individual racism and institutional racism respectively. The first consists of overt acts by individuals which cause death, injury, or the violent destruction of property. This type can be reached by television cameras; it can frequently be observed in the process of commission. The second type is less overt, far more subtle, less identifiable in terms of specific individuals committing the acts. But it is no less destructive of human life. The second type

originates in the operation of established and re-
spected forces in the society, and thus receives far
less public condemnation than the first type. [1]

The Kerner Report observed the separateness in this
country, and presented solutions which needed to be taken
to lessen the racial conflict in this country. [2] While the
report made a strong indictment of white racism, it did
not rest the responsibility for the sordid conditions of
black Americans upon the white institutions.

Because institutional racism is a relatively recent concept, there is only a small amount of related literature.
Hopefully this study will provide an analytical framework for further examination of institutional racism.

Carmichael and Hamilton coined the term "institutional racism," outlined the forms it takes, and suggested ways of dealing with the problem. During the
civil rights movement, they urged that blacks adopt a
different political framework and ideology for this society
to work out its racial problems. [3] They encouraged a
new consciousness as a sense of peoplehood. Pride, an
attitude of brotherly, communal responsibility among all
black people is to be the first order of business. They refer
to this as "political modernization." It is the first step in
the process of the elimination of racism.

According to Carmichael and Hamilton, political modernization includes three major concepts: (1) questioning
old values and institutions of society; (2) searching for new
and different forms of political structure to solve political
and economic problems; and (3) broadening the base of
political participation to include more people in the
decision-making process. [4] The development of organizations of black social workers, health service workers,
teachers, policemen, lawyers, churchmen, and various dis-
ciplinary caucuses are related to Carmichael's and Hamil-

ton's first point: questioning old values and institutions of the society. These groups reflect their suggestion that

> blacks must re-define themselves and reclaim their own history, their culture; create their own sense of community and togetherness. Group solidarity is necessary before a group can operate effectively from a bargaining position in a pluralistic society. [5]

Key's work on special interest groups is related to these newly formed black professional groups. [6] These groups, as part of the current political socialization, can help to combat institutional racism. According to Key, a new group sets off political movement by raising questions that challenge the very nature of society—values, beliefs, and institutions. Actions among black professionals in challenging the established institutions do reflect this trend.

Kerner also developed a strong indictment of white racism but did not deal substantively with the race questions or the causes of civil disorders as an institutional force. [7] Said the report: "White society is deeply implicated in the ghetto, and white society condones it." The report's recommendations are directed at ghetto conditions, and not the white structures, practices, or policies which are responsible for much of the racial problem. Recommendations were also stated in terms of improving communications, while fuller presentation and analysis of oppressive institutional policies and practices should have been encouraged.

Nevertheless, the report opened up for redefinition the "Negro problem." It moved from concentration upon the victims to clearer perceptions of the oppressors. White racism was now to receive some priority in view of its contributions to the racial crisis in this country.

The most definitive discussion of institutional racism yet to appear has been the Knowles and Prewitt book. [8] It deals with the arrangements and practices among health, education, justice, economic, and political institutions which are at the base of black rebellion. By living in the black community, the contributors to that book documented frequent and specific examples of subtle institutional racist practices. They showed that reform of white institutions will correct many of the inequities in institutional racism.

Knowles and Prewitt reveal an insightful picture of the racist actions and structures of health care institutions. In a chapter entitled, "Why White Americans Are Healthier," we gain a view of the inferior health of black people in this country. Indicators of this are: higher mortality rates for blacks, poor routine immunization, participation in public indigent services which are unequal, racist individual and institutional medical education system.

> . . . to say that health care is an economic not a racial issue is to overlook irrefutable evidence to the contrary. If the education, labor and business institutions make it difficult for blacks to earn a decent living, medicine has helped perpetuate institutional racism by rationing health care according to ability to pay, by providing inadequate and inferior health care for poor people, and by failing to establish structures which can meet health needs in ways acceptable to all patients. [9]

The authors provide us with solutions to institutional racism, following their rather comprehensive examination of the topic. They propose various anti-racist activities such as: development of multicultural curriculums, selective home purchasing, consumer education, black self-determination, and examination of institutional policies. Specific issues must be dealt with. Commitment to the premise that "institutions made by men can be changed by men" is only part of their suggested scheme.

An increasing amount of literature continues to be developed on the subject of white racism. While most of it does not deal specifically with institutional racism, it is applicable to the topic because most institutions and organizations have been organized and controlled from a white perspective. The U.S. Commission on Civil Rights recently prepared a booklet, *Racism in America and How to Combat It*. [10] Mention is made of the invisibility of institutional subordination. The term refers to the geographic exclusion of minority group members from all-white areas; of perceptual distortion in the way people see reality.

Examples of institutional subordination include: absence of non-whites from white residential areas; creation of new jobs in suburban areas; zoning laws which discourage housing for relatively lower-income groups; and de facto residential segregation.

The dynamics of institutional subordination produce racist effects from acts which are usually not overtly racist in either content or intention. Racist actions are embedded in the institutional context when they are

> directly linked to other actions that are overtly racist (such as basing employment policies on acceptance of unions that deliberately exclude Negro members);
>
> heavily reliant upon personal qualifications of skills which minority group members have not been permitted to achieve because of past overt racism (such as requiring passage of academically oriented tests for getting a job, or basing early ability group-

ing of children in public schools on tests administered only in English in areas where many children
have been reared in Spanish-speaking homes);

dependent upon institutional arrangements which
embody the residual results of past overt
racism. [11]

One of the most recent discussions of institutional
racism is that of Wilcox. He speaks of the failures of the
white community to combat white institutional racism.
Little has been done to eradicate racism or transfer control
of the black community. Wilcox sees social policy as social
control. Shapers of public policy find ways to hide from
their own racism and perpetuate black colonialism. Wilcox
outlines several approaches for blacks to gain control of
their communities. These include: (1) blacks must make
decisions about the lives of black people; (2) blacks must
determine who speaks for the black community; (3) black
communities must involve themselves in collecting and
interpreting data so as to insure greater congruence between public policies and needs of the black community;
(4) blacks must acquire the means to restructure the socio-
economic relationship between themselves and the broader
community. [12]

In the last few years, various literature has appeared on
white racism, but perusal of the literature reveals that
specific documentation of institutional racism is nonexistent. We will attempt to compensate for the lack by
presenting documentation and insights in this relatively
virgin field of inquiry.

Purpose of the Study. We have conducted our research
with these objectives: (1) to explore the patterns of institutional racism among established, predominantly white

professional organizations, as perceived by leaders in newly-formed black professional organizations; (2) to identify the tactics used by the black groups to deal with racism; (3) to analyze the effectiveness of the strategies developed by these new ethnic-based organizations; and (4) to discuss the implications of this experience for future actions by black professionals.

During the past several years, a number of new professional interest groups have developed among black professionals. [13] The primary aims of these organizations are: strengthening the inner black community, building a power base, and reducing their own alienation and powerlessness. But more important for this study, these groups have questioned the national, white, established, professional organizations because of their patterns of institutional racism. They perceive many of the organizational practices and policies as racist. Some of these practices involve: staffing patterns; role and function; organizational values; membership; lack of representation of minority group content in education and training programs, publications, conferences, and program activity; scholarships and awards; recruitment; funding sources; official positions on social issues; and coalitions, among other patterns.

Based on the increasing independent efforts to form black professional organizations to deal with institutional racism, our study seeks answers to the following questions:

What were the perceptions by leaders of emerging black professional organizations of institutional racism in established white professional organizations?

In developing their own professional organizations, what were the strategies used by black professionals to deal with their perceptions?

How effective have the strategies been in developing the organizations?

Research Methodology. This study is primarily an exploratory, descriptive, comparative approach to the study of perceptions of institutional racism by leaders of newly-formed black professional organizations between 1967 and 1970. While there are some twenty or more national, black, professional organizations, we selected only two national groups which were formed during this time. [14]

This study deals with the *perceptions* held by leaders rather than an empirical examination of the organizations, because it is interested in basic reasons for the formation of the new groups. Their perception of forms of racism reveals what the black professionals were questioning about the established white organizations. To perceive a reaction is to feel it and believe it. We were not intersted in logical, proven evidence of racism but in its perceptions, whose study can give a more accurate interpretation of the feelings and attitudes of these black professionals. It supports the basis for protest, which was fervent in the black community during the times the groups emerged. It is not sufficient to say that national white professional organizations were integrated because there was a physical mixture of blacks and whites. But rather we must ask, What did the blacks *feel* and *believe*? Did they feel that the organization coincided with their needs and interests? Were the organizations legitimate in terms of blacks sharing benefits? There was a growing alienation among the blacks in these groups. Our focus on their perceptions gives a better indication of their *faith* in and *reactions* to white professional associations.

NABSW and NAHSE. The National Association of Black Social Workers (NABSW) and the National Association of

Health Services Executives (NAHSE) are independent, ethnic-based groups rather than in-house protest organizations within the predominantly white, national associations. While these groups started during the period under study, they are significant because these professions also include a preponderance of blacks in the areas of welfare and human service, in which most blacks are employed. [15] These groups then best typify those that represent public services and professional interests.

NABSW is a national, nonprofit organization, founded in 1967, with chapters in Alabama, California, Connecticut, the District of Columbia, Florida, Georgia, Illinois, Indiana, Kansas, Maryland, Massachusetts, Michigan, Mississippi, Missouri, New Jersey, New York, North Carolina, Ohio, Oklahoma, Pennsylvania, and South Carolina. All chapters are represented on the National Steering Committee. The general membership is approximately 1,000 members. Currently there is no paid staff, and the budget is estimated at $25,000. Headquarters are located in New York City. Annual meetings and conferences are sponsored.

NAHSE is a national, nonprofit, tax-exempt, association of black health service administrators. Organized in November 1967 in New York, its membership includes a variety of specialists who hold decision-making positions in the health fields, such as hospital administrators, physicians, and non-credential administrative personnel. Chapters are based in California, Illinois, Maryland, and New York. The general membership totals approximately 200 members. There is a current budget of $15,000 with no paid staff. The budget is primarily based on the dues structure. Annual meetings, conferences, and a national work-study, recruitment program are offered.

The national, white, professional associations perceived

by black professionals as having racist patterns consist of at least five groups. These perceptions among black social work leaders pertained to the National Association of Social Workers, National Conference on Social Welfare, and Council on Social Work Education; and among black health administrators pertained to the American Hospital Association and the American College of Hospital Administrators.

NASW. The National Association of Social Workers is a national, nonprofit organization whose primary purpose is to improve practice and extend knowledge in the field of social work. Its national professional membership consists of 50,000 members, with a national staff of some 60 people. Publications consist of *Abstracts for Social Workers, NASW News and Personnel Information,* and the *Journal of Social Work.* There are 173 chapters in 50 states.

NCSW. The National Conference on Social Welfare is a voluntary organization of 10,000 individual and organizational members. Founded in 1873, its major function is to provide a national forum for the critical examination of basic problems and issues in the field of social welfare. Its national headquarters are in Columbus, Ohio. The NCSW serves as a base for state conferences in social welfare; as secretariat for the U.S. Committee of the International Council on Social Welfare; and as a clearinghouse for educational materials for use on local, state, national, and international levels. [16]

CSWE. The Council on Social Work Education provides leadership and service to social work education in the United States and Canada. Its major responsibility is the accreditation of schools of social work granting master's degrees in social work. Services are available through consultation, conferences, publications, and special projects. At the time of our study, membership included 72 graduate schools of social work; 218 colleges and universities with undergraduate social welfare programs; 46 national, voluntary, and governmental social agencies; NASW and Canadian Association of Social Workers; and the National Federation of Student Social Workers. Associate membership included 15 graduate schools working toward accreditation; 381 libraries; 294 local social and health agencies; 3,552 individual and 116 international members. Periodicals and publications include journals, newsletters, reports, books and teaching materials. [17]

AHA. The American Hospital Association, founded in 1898, is a national organization whose object is to promote the public welfare through the development of better hospital care for all people. Its major source of income is from its member organizations. Membership categories include institutional, associate, and personal. During our study, the organization had some 17,000 members and its staff included 350 personnel, and had an annual budget for operating of $500,000. Its publication is a semi-monthly journal, *Hospitals.* The annual meeting in 1971 was held in Chicago. [18]

ACHA. The American College of Hospital Administrators, founded in 1933, is the professional accrediting body for establishing and maintaining standards of hospital administration. Publications include a directory and a journal, *Hospital Administration.* The annual conference was held in San Francisco during 1971. The annual budget was over one million dollars. [19]

The perceptions of institutional racism by the two black groups can provide a constructive overview of black professionals' reaction to racist patterns. Also more elaborate data in several instances will allow for meaningful generalizations and conceptual strategies to develop in relation to the current profusion of emerging black interest groups. [20] Both organizations were compared as to the similarities and differences among the perceptions of institutional racism and as to the strategies used to deal with racism. The use of comparison groups focusing on a single problem is of value as a means of surmounting the limitations of a single case study. [21]

A personal, unstructured interview was held with interviewees from each selected black professional organization. The sample group for this study consisted of national officers, and members of the national steering committee or board of directors. This amount to fifteen interviews per national black professional organization.

Because the sample group included national officers or steering committee members who are located in various geographical areas, interviews were confined to those leaders who lived in Chicago, the Baltimore-Washington area, or New York. Leaders who were interviewed could have been either officers or, in the case of NABSW, members of the national steering committee. It also included some leaders who held office in either 1969 or 1970. National officers for NABSW consisted of the following: National President, National Vice President, National Secretary, and National Treasurer. The national steering committee included, other than elected officers, two representatives per chapter and one per state. National officers for NAHSE included the President, President Elect, First Vice President, Treasurer, Secretary, Corresponding Secretary, Parliamentarian, three members of the Executive Board, Committee Chairman, and a Past President.

An interview schedule, which appears in Figure 1, was devised and administered by the investigator. This schedule

Figure 1

INTERVIEW SCHEDULE

Purpose of Interview:

To obtain black professionals' perceptions of institutional racism in established, national, white, professional organizations.

Problem:

How did leaders of emerging, black, professional organizations perceive the institutional racism in established, national, white, professional organizations?
Ask lead questions, using open-ended approach:

1. What forms of racism exist in these white organizations?
2. What have you done about it?
3. How effective have the strategies been?
4. Why or why not effective?
5. What were the basic reasons for forming the black professional organization?

Specific Questions:

I. *Perceptions dealing with internal administration of the organization:*

What do you see as an indication or pattern of institutional racism in these white organizations prior to beginning of NAHSE or NABSW?

What was the strategy used in attacking *each* pattern?

1. *Staffing Pattern*

What was the staffing pattern's racial distribution in relation to policy-making positions among the following:

   a) Board
   b) Chairmanship of boards and committees (leadership)
   c) Consultants, officers, or managers

2. *Role and Function of the Organization*

   What was the role, function, or purpose of the organization(s)? Does the organization role or purpose serve the interest of black people?

3. *Organizational Ideology*

   Has the organization operationalized its values and principles?

4. *Membership*

   What has been the number of blacks in the organization?

5. *Goals*

   What was the organization's goal? Does it serve the interest of black people?

6. *Program Activity*

   What programs have been conducted to meet the needs of blacks? Have programs been set up deliberately to meet the needs of blacks?

7. *Publications (journals, newsletters, other media)*

   To what degree did the organization's publications reflect materials on blacks or inclusion of black authors?

8. *Conferences*

   To what extent were blacks represented at professional conferences? (Include information regarding topics, participation as speakers or on panels, and attendance.)

9. *Benefits*

Has the organization sponsored scholarships, fellowships, or grants for research or professional education of blacks?

10. *Recruitment*

What has the organization done in the recruitment of blacks to the profession or to the staff?

11. *Funding Source*

What were the funding sources of the institution or organization? How do these financial sources relate to the issues of institutional racism?

12. *Evaluation*

What are the criteria by which the organization evaluates its success or failure? How do they relate to its aims and services?

II. *Perceptions dealing with policies, legislation, and lobbies:*

1. *Official Position and Social Action*

Has the organization taken an active position on major social issues affecting minority groups? What has the organization done to respect the black position?

2. *Coalitions and Alliances*

In what ways has the organization used its influence to affect other institutional policies regarding minority groups?

III. *Since the imitiation of the black organization, have you perceived any racist principles of the organization?*

IV. *How has the black organization adapted itself to the charge of institutional racism?*

provided a guide for depth-probing regarding the black professionals' perceptions of institutional racism in a parallel national, white, established, professional organization. It also secured data regarding strategies used to deal with the racism. A frequency scale on forms of institutional racism was also devised (see Figure 2). This device provided a measurement of fifteen manifestations of racism. Appointments for interviews were prearranged by letter and telephone after approval of this research activity by the national presidents. Interviews were conducted intermittently over a five-month period.

The interviews were taped in order to secure more accurate and precise information, feelings, and tones of the interviewees. After transcription of the tapes, the responses were analyzed and coded according to the classifications scheme on racist patterns among the predominantly white, established associations and the strategies to deal with racism which have been developed by the newly-formed groups.

Records, documents, files, reports, program activities and conference agenda of the organizations over a three-year period were also reviewed. All these sources provided data for review and analysis of the perceptions of institutional racism.

Data from the depth interviews, records, reports, and other documents were collected. An analysis was made of the data. This exploratory, descriptive, comparative study is a micro-analysis that certainly will lead to certain assumptions or theories about black professional organizations.

Preliminary Study: NCBPS. So that we could empirically generate categories of racism as well as to sharpen the experimental instruments, a pre-test study was conducted. A sample group of similar characteristics was selected and

Figure 2

FREQUENCY SCALE OF INDICATORS
OF INSTITUTIONAL RACISM

The following scale is constructed as a device for measuring the frequency of indicators of institutional racism in established, white, national, professional organizations. (Check as indicated in the interview.)

    — Staffing Pattern
    — Role and Function
    — Organizational Ideology
    — Membership
    — Goals
    — Program Activity
    — Publications
    — Conferences
    — Fringe Benefits (scholarships, awards)
    — Recruitment
    — Funding Source
    — Official Position on Social Issues
    — Coalitions

fifty percent of this group was interviewed. The National Conference of Black Political Scientists, another newly-formed black professional group, was selected for this pre-test. The findings of this preliminary study of eight leaders in the NCBPS are discussed in the Appendix.

Delimitations of the Study. This study concerns itself primarily with newly-formed black professional organizations. Three years are a relatively short time span for the initial development of national organizations.

This study is concerned only with differential responses of black professional organizations to the areas of patterns of institutional racism, and strategies and their effectiveness in dealing with the racism. The evidence of black nationalist doctrine, the means of dissolving neutrality of administrative systems or reform of professional criteria are all possible areas of further study of newly-formed black professional organizations.

This study of the perceptions of institutional racism concerns itself with data from the individual subjects. Presumably, the leadership of such organizations is representative of the membership.

There are always certain limitations and biases in any study. The investigator, who is a black professional, recognized that his own interests in the black professional movement played an important part in the selection of this topic.

Definition of Terms. A number of terms need to be operationally defined for the purpose of this study:

> *newly-formed, black, professional organization* refers to an ethnic-based, national, nonprofit, cooperative, voluntary organization composed of black persons with the same occupational interests. The organization would have started during the period between 1967 and 1970.

> *established, white, professional organization* refers to a national, nonprofit, cooperative, voluntary association or occupational area which has been in existence for at least ten years.

> *institutional racism* refers to the covert, subtle form of racism which originates in the operation of established and respected forces in the society; the act occurs without the presence of conscious bigotry. This term is now used also in the sense of *institutional subordination*—referring to the action,

attitudes, or institutional structures which subordinate a person or group because of his or their color. [22]

public services refers to institutions, programs, and employees in large-scale public organizations.

public administration refers to the professional study and practice aimed at improving administration of public service at all levels of government. A modest number of these persons are products of professional schools. [23]

perception refers, for the purposes of this study, to an awareness of sensory stimulation in which attitudes are formed in relationship to self, objects, and environmental stimulation. Because of the cognitive components of its formation, there exists an enduring state of readiness to stimuli, objects, persons' social values, and cultural norms [24]. Here the word *perception* related durably to the black professional's belief that an organization's values coincide with the values and aspirations of black people. [25]

black professional refers, for the purpose of this study, to a black person irrespective of credentials whose occupational activity is serving a client's needs and solving his problems. The definition of professional corresponds to that of Dumont in which he identified the following characteristics: responsive to citizens, indifferent to credentials with a sense of superordinate purpose, critically oriented to change, and driven by compassion. [26]

leaders refers to those persons elected to office to exert special direction and guidance to an emerging black professional organization. They have a special influence over the majority of members, and are representative of members' needs and attitudes. [27]

NOTES

1. Stokely S. Carmichael and Charles V. Hamilton, *Black Power: The Politics of Liberation in America* (New York: Random House, 1967), pp. 4-6.

2. National Advisory Commission on Civil Disorders, *Report of the National Advisory Commission on Civil Disorders* (New York: Bantam Books, 1968), p. 10.

3. Carmichael and Hamilton, *ibid.,* p. 4.

4. *Ibid.,* p. 39.

5. *Ibid.,* p. 44.

6. V. O. Key, Jr., *Politics, Parties, and Pressure Groups,* (New York: Crowell Company, 5th ed., 1964), p. 57.

7. National Advisory Commission on Civil Disorders, *ibid.,* pp. 203-6.

8. Louis L. Knowles and Kenneth Prewitt, eds., *Institutional Racism in America* (Englewood Cliffs, N.J.: Prentice-Hall, Inc., 1968), p. 59.

9. *Ibid.,* p. 105.

10. U.S. Commission on Civil Rights, *Racism in America and How to Combat It,* (Washington, D.C.: Government Printing Office, 1970).

11. *Ibid.,* p. 16.

12. Preston Wilcox, "Social Policy and White Racism," *Social Policy,* (May-June 1970), pp. 41-46.

13. Charles L. Sanders, "Growth of Associations of Black Social Workers," *Social Casework,* LI (May 1970), pp. 277-84.

14. Charles L. Sanders, "Black Assertion Among Black Professionals," *Journal of National Medical Association,* Vol. 63, (November 1971), p. 460.

15. *Ibid.*

16. *The Social Welfare Forum, National Conference on Social Welfare, 1970* (New York: Columbia University Press, 1970), p. vii.

17. *Service Directory of National Organizations,* ed., Louise Numan, (New York: National Assembly for Social Policy and Development, Inc., 1969), p. 41.

18. *1970 Directory of National Trade and Professional Associations of the United States,* ed., Craig Colgate, Jr., (Washington, D.C.: Columbia Books, Inc.), p. 36.

19. *Ibid.,* p. 30.

20. Herbert Kaufman, "The Next Step in Case Studies," *Public Administration Review,* XVII (Winter 1958), pp. 52-59.

21. *Ibid.,* pp. 52-59. Bernard Berelson and Gary A. Steiner, *Human Behavior: An Inventory of Scientific Findings,* (New York: Harcourt, Brace and World, Inc., 1964), p. 27. Harold Stein, *Public Administration and Policy Development: A Case Book,* (New York: Harcourt, Brace and World, Inc., 1952), p. xxxviii.

22. Carmichael and Hamilton, *Black Power: The Politics of Liberation in America, op. cit.,* p. 4. Knowles and Prewitt, *Institutional Racism in America, op. cit.,* p. 1. U.S. Commission on Civil Rights, *Racism in America and How to Combat It, op. cit.*

23. John C. Honey, "Higher Education for Public Service," *Public Administration Review,* XXVII (November 1967), pp. 294-321.

24. Gardner Murphy, *Personality,* (New York: Harper and Bros., 1947). William H. Ileson and Hadley Cantril, *Perception: A Transitional Approach,* (New York: Doubleday and Co., Inc., 1954). Muzafer Sherif and Hadley Cantril, *The Psychology of Ego Involvement,* (New York: John Wiley and Sons, 1947).

25. Seymour Lipset, *Political Man,* (New York: Doubleday and Co., Inc., 1960). Seymour Lipset, *The First New Nation,* (New York: Anchor Books, 1967).

26. Matthew P. Dumont, "The Changing Face of Professionalism," *Social Policy,* (May/June 1970), p. 26.

27. Emory S. Bogardus, *Leaders and Leadership,* (New York: Appleton-Century Company, 1934), p. 12. Hugh H. Smythe, "Changing Patterns in Negro Leadership," *Social Forces,* XXIX, (December 1950).

2 | Comparative Characteristics of the Black Leaders Surveyed

ALTHOUGH THE SAMPLE GROUPS were described generally in the methodology, answers must be given to several basic questions: Who are the leaders? What part do they play in the organization? Is there a relationship between the characteristics of the group, the perceptions, and strategies? We hope to find answers from our findings on characteristics of the leaders.

Age. The social work leaders were younger than the health administrators. None of the social work leaders was in the age category 50-59, whereas this was the largest age category for the health administrators.

This age differential might be expected because health administration is a specialty, requires experience in the medical-health field. Administrative careers also tend to be associated with the more experienced and skilled person, who more than likely would be older (see Table 1 on age distribution). This trend, however, is changing as blacks move more readily into administrative jobs at a younger age. For example, in Norfolk, Virginia and New Orleans, Louisiana, there are black hospitals being administered by persons under 30 years of age. In addition, those who are in the field have had little opportunity to attract younger

Figure 3

QUESTIONNAIRE ON CHARACTERISTICS
OF BLACK PROFESSIONAL LEADERS

1. Age:
   ☐ 20-39 ☐ 40-49
   ☐ 30-39 ☐ 50-59

2. Sex:
   ☐ Male
   ☐ Female

3. Education and Training and Location:
   Undergraduate College: 1, 2, 3, 4 (Circle one)
   Where?
   Graduate school and location:

4. Marital Status:
   ☐ Married ☐ Divorced ☐ Separated
   ☐ Single ☐ Widowed ☐ Other

5. Length of time in Profession:
   ☐ Less than 2 years ☐ Over 5 years
   ☐ Less than 4 years ☐ Over 10 years

6. Do you belong to a white established professional organization? Yes_____ No_____

7. Length of time in established white professional organization:
   ☐ Less than 2 years ☐ Over 5 years
   ☐ Less than 4 years ☐ Over 10 years

8. If you do not belong to a white established group, why not?

9. Length of time in office of Black Professional association:

10. Current Job Position:

blacks into the profession. Another reason for the difference may be attributed to the fact that social work as a career has been better known to blacks, and younger graduates have known that they can secure employment in this field.

Sex. Both groups of leaders were primarily male. The social worker group had a larger proportion of females than the health administrator group.

These results might be expected since leadership and administration tend to imply a need for aggressiveness and, culturally, this characteristic has been attributed to males. Among the social work group there was a conscious effort to project the black male into a leadership role. This period of black consciousness, in which there was emphasis on building more positive male images and rejecting myths such as predominance of a matricentric or female-dominated culture among black people, made this desirable. Although there are more opportunities for women in social work, there were fewer females in this category (see Table 2 on sex distribution).

Table 1

AGE LEVELS OF BLACK SOCIAL WORKERS
AND HEALTH ADMINISTRATORS

Social Workers		Health Administrators	
Age	*Percent*	*Age*	*Percent*
30-39	60	50-59	40
20-29	27	40-49	33
40-49	13	30-39	27
Total	100	Total	100

Table 2

SEX

Sex	Social Workers Percent	Health Administrators Percent
Male	80	93
Female	20	7
Total	100	100

Marital Status. Among the two groups, the health administrators were predominantly a married group. The social workers had a higher proportion of single, divorced, or separated individuals. This could be attributed to the fact that the social workers were a younger group, whereas hospital administrators were older, more settled, and stabilized in their careers and personal lives (see Table 3 on marital status).

Table 3

MARITAL STATUS

Marital Status	Social Workers Percent	Health Administrators Percent
Married	60	93
Single	20	—
Divorced	13	—
Separated	7	7
Total	100	100

Table 4

EDUCATIONAL LEVELS

Educational Level	Social Workers *Percent*	Health Administrators *Percent*
Undergraduate	100	93
No formal training	–	7
Total	100	100
Graduate	100	87
No formal training	–	13
Total	100	100

Education, Training, and Location. All of the social workers and health administrators were college graduates. This is because professional social work and health management requires master's degree level graduate training. The social workers had been educated on the college level at both Southern, black colleges and Northern colleges and universities. The health administrators had mostly received their college level training at Southern, black colleges, probably due to the fact that since they were older, this was the only opportunity available to them. Both groups received graduate training primarily in the North or Midwest. There had been no graduate training program in hospital administration in the South to accommodate black students (see Table 4 on educational levels and Table 5 on location of educational institutions).

Length of Time in the Profession. When the two groups are compared, the social workers were relative newcomers

Table 5

REGIONAL LOCATION OF EDUCATIONAL INSTITUTIONS

Location Undergraduate School	Social Workers Percent	Health Administrators Percent
Northern	50	6
Southern	40	87
Midwest	10	–
None	–	7
Total	100	100

Graduate School		
Northern	80	40
Southern	10	7
Midwest	10	40
None	–	13
Total	100	100

to the profession. Most of the health administrators had been in the field for more than 10 years, whereas this was the smallest group among the social workers. Again, this is probably attributable to the age differential.

As indicated earlier, black students have not been oriented to management careers. Traditionally, blacks have been attracted to teaching, preaching, and social work. The decade of the 60's saw an upsurge of younger blacks entering the human services field. In fact, the National Association of Black Social Workers was conceived and inspired by students. Consequently, one might expect the younger group to be relatively new to the profession, and among the first black professionals to challenge social welfare establishments (see Table 6 on length of time in the profession). [1]

Membership in White Association. A larger percentage, 80 percent, of black health administrators belong to white, established, professional, health associations. Sixty-nine percent of the black social workers had membership in the white, established, professional social work associations. This finding might be expected in view of the age difference and less traditional or bureaucratic orientation and professional orientation among the social workers, especially those who are client oriented (see Table 7 and Tables 8A and 8B on membership in white professional associations). [2]

Length of Time in White Association. When the two groups were compared, the health administrators had held membership in the white groups for a longer period of time. Eighty percent had membership over a ten-year period, whereas the percentage for social workers was 13 percent for the same period of time. The largest number of social workers, 27 percent, held membership for a period

Table 6

LENGTH OF TIME IN PROFESSION

Time in Years	Social Workers *Percent*	Health Administrators *Percent*
Less than 5	33	—
5-9	47	20
10 or more	20	80
Total	100	100

Table 7

MEMBERSHIP IN NATIONAL, WHITE, ESTABLISHED,
PROFESSIONAL ASSOCIATIONS

Membership	Social Worker *Percent*	Health Administrators *Percent*
Member	60	80
Non-member	40	20
Total	100	100

of less than four years; while 13 percent of the health administrators held membership for the same period of time (see Table 9 on length of time in white professional association).

Reason for Non-Membership. The health administrators, when questioned as to their reason for not belonging to a white, established group, indicated that it was not relevant to health problems of their interest, nor did the organizations personally benefit them. The social workers responded primarily to the association's role and ideology, questioning whether or not it was a legitimate institution because of its "eliteness" and irrelevancy to contemporary issues affecting black people.

Table 8A

BLACK WORKER MEMBERSHIP IN
NATIONAL ASSOCIATION OF SOCIAL WORKERS

Membership	*Percent*
Members	.60
Non-Members	.40
Total	.100

Table 8B

BLACK HEALTH ADMINISTRATOR
MEMBERSHIP IN AMERICAN COLLEGE
OF HOSPITAL ADMINISTRATORS

Membership	*Percent*
Members	.47
Fellows	.33
Nominees or non-affiliated	.20
Total	.100

Those administrators who did not belong to the white group were not really questioning their premises, purposes or goals, perhaps because their exclusion from the group precluded active scrutiny and involvement.

Length of Time in Black Association. Among the two groups of leaders, the health administrators, 67 percent, had been members of this group for a longer period of

Table 9

LENGTH OF TIME IN NATIONAL, WHITE,
ESTABLISHED, PROFESSIONAL ASSOCIATION

Time in Years	Social Worker *Percent*	Health Administrator *Percent*
Less than 2	7	—
2-4	27	—
5-9	13	13
10 or more	13	80
Non-affiliated	40	7
Total	100	100

time than the social workers, 20 percent. While the health administrators had been in the organization longer, the social worker leaders included a number of persons other than those who founded the organization. This is attributed to the fact that there are many more black social workers than black health administrators. [3] In fact, black health administrators are almost nonexistent. According to an NAHSE report there are more than 7,000 hospitals in the United States, and there are only 38 blacks affiliated with the American College of Hospital Administrators. There were 45 blacks enrolled in schools of hospital administration in 1970-71, out of a total student enrollment in excess of 1,700. [4] (See Table 10.)

Current Job Positions. When the two groups of leaders are compared, both are not only leaders in their respective organizations, but currently hold high level positions. The health administrators were all top-level decision-makers.

Style of Leadership. Although this study deals with a large group of leaders, there are ways in which individuals distinguished themselves in terms of developing a new organization. This was particularly noticeable when the thrust for all-black groups represented a phenomenon in the black community. Because black people are undergoing individual and collective change in relation to becoming black oriented, it was found that the leaders played different roles. Blacks have been either anti-black, brainwashed, or "colored" in their perspectives, but find themselves having become Afro-American, Pan-Africanists, or simply black as they traversed the stages in the Negro-to-black conversion experience. [5]

As we try to interpret here what the leaders were like and how they acted, we mirror our impressions against a number of stereotypes about the educated, well-to-do,

Table 10

LENGTH OF TIME IN BLACK PROFESSIONAL ASSOCIATION

Time in Years	Social Worker *Percent*	Health Administrator *Percent*
2	80	—
3	20	100
Total	100	100

black militant or black middle class. There have also been many ways of referring to the styles and types of leadership. Such traditional concepts as individualistic, authoritarian, weak, strong, democratic, literalistic, charismatic, bureaucratic, "middle of the road," radical, and conservative are often used. However, the situational nature of leadership is considered here, because of the leaders involved from the political setting, time, and values inherent in this period of protest and crises. [6]

Three patterns of leadership emerged, as the varied functions performed by the leaders were analyzed. Because these are leaders, the categories are somewhat more pure than if the general membership had been analyzed. The three types of leaders are: organizer or activist, implementer or sustainer, and supportive. For the most part, these are considered forms of behavior, representing groups of leaders who play some part in coordinating and motivating individuals and groups to achieve the desired end of their respective organizations (see Tables 11A and 11B).

Leader Type: Organizer or Activist. Refers to those leaders who raise issues, create, and direct the organization

Table 11A

TYPE OF LEADERSHIP ROLES
AMONG BLACK SOCIAL WORKERS

Role*   *Percent*

Role*	Percent
Activists	.87
Non-activists	.13
Total	100
Implementer	.73
Non-implementer	.27
Total	100

*The social worker role was dual-type leadership in which they were both organizers and implementers.

toward its goals. This is the person who initiates or stimulates the action. The organizer contributes time, energy, money, and reputation to the new organization. This is the person who has the more militant qualities.

Leader Type: Implementer or Sustainer. Refers to those leaders who provide continuity and follow-through with much of the action or plans stimulated by the activists.

Table 11B

TYPE OF LEADERSHIP ROLES
AMONG BLACK HEALTH ADMINISTRATORS

Role	Percent
Activists	.50
Implementers	.23
Supporters	.27
Total	100

Because of minimal resources and scarce leadership abilities in the black community, the activists and implementers often overlap. Noticeable also, is the fact that the organizers who wear the new badge of "blackness" may end up as sustainers because of their high level of commitment. This is the person committed to a plan. He is trying to change his community. This is the person who has internalized a high degree of commitment to black values and institutions.

Leader Type: Supportive. Refers to those leaders who simply provide their knowledge or prestige, moral encouragement, and membership finances. The supporter is the moderate individual as compared to the more militant organizer.

Among the social work leaders, approximately 87 percent could be described as organizers or activists. These were the people who have been involved as early founders of the organization; representatives of NABSW in major confrontations with white established groups; planning and setting up the national conferences; organizing and soliciting recruits; chairing meetings; and providing seed money for the initial organization, among many other activities.

Among this same group of leaders, at least 73 percent might be described as implementers or sustainers. That is, out of the 15 leaders, only four of them did not fulfill the criteria as organizers. In most instances, the organizers became implementers because they had best presented an idea, were knowledgeable or able to give direction to a plan. Also, the scarcity of manpower and resources for projects and plans usually induced the organizers to become implementers.

The health administrators as a group of leaders played different roles from the social worker leaders. Whereas the social workers were a much more assertive and implementing group on the whole, the health administrators were rather evenly divided as activists and implementers. Half of the group were innovators for change in the health care system; the other half were were implementers. About 23 percent of the implementers were persons who were not a part of the activists. About 27 percent of the health administrators could be defined as supporters. Because the health administrators were an older group who were less inclined to deal directly with black activism as a philosophical concept, and because so many of their years had been spent in being like "whites" or pushing for integration, these health professionals offered primarily their prestige and status as national black health figures.

NOTES

1. Howard E. Prunty, "The New York Story—A Participant's Viewpoint," *Social Welfare Forum, 1969,* (New York: Columbia University Press), pp. 185-192. Charles L. Sanders, "Growth of the Association of Black Social Workers," *Social Casework,* Vol. 51, (May 1970), pp. 277-84.

2. Irwin Epstein, "Professional Role Orientation and Conflict Strategies," *Social Work,* (October 1970), pp. 87-92. Andrew Billingsley, "Bureaucratic and Professional Orientation Pattern in Social Casework," *Social Service Review,* Vol. 4, (December 1964), pp. 400-07. Harold L. Wilensky and Charles N. Lebeaux, *Industrial Society and Social Welfare,* 2nd ed., (New York: Free Press, 1965).

3. Alfred M. Stamm, "NASW Membership: Characteristics, Deployment and Salaries," *Personnel Information,* XII, National Association of Social Workers, (May 1969), p. 35.

4. Position paper: "Partners in the Health Care System," National Association of Health Service Executives, (March 1971). (Mimeographed)

5. William Cross, Jr., "The Negro-to-Black Conversion Experience," *Black World,* Vol. XX, (July 1971), pp. 13-27.

6. John N. Pfiffner and Robert Presthus, *Public Administration,* 5th ed., (New York: Ronald Press, 1967), pp. 87-94.

3 | A Typology of Institutional Racism

BEFORE THE VARIOUS INDICATORS of racism are reported, some discussion of each might better explain their different perceptions among the leaders. Any organization has various parts or dimensions. As a deliberately constructed social unit which seeks specific goals, the organization as a social unit has a series of patterns or entities. [1] For the purpose of analyzing an organization, we developed fifteen dimensions and characteristics which are likely to be found in a professional association. The same dimensions, when analyzed, reveal forms of racism. The organization was divided into patterns relative to internal administration and those relative to external administration, such as lobbies and coalitions. The forms of racism might be identified by looking at the fifteen facets: Staffing, Role and Function (purpose), Values framework, Membership, Goals, Program, Publications, Conferences, Recruitment, Funding Source, Evaluation, Scholarships and Awards, Education and Training, Official Positions on Social Issues, and Coalitions and Alliances.

Our analysis of racist indicators was based upon the results of the pre-test and is not cited as a final, or pure form but merely a practical one for studying the racist patterns in an organization. With the increasing indictments against racist organizations, it is important to analyze how racism manifests itself in an organization. Other frameworks for organizational or institutional analysis have been offered by other theorists. Malinowksi's classification uses the following points: (1) charter, (2) personnel, (3) norms, (4) material apparatus, (5) activities, and (6) function. [2] Etzioni rejects the focus on goals as an approach to system models.

> . . . Rather than comparing existing organizations to ideals of what they might be, we may assess performance relative to one another . . . The system model constitutes a statement about relationships which must exist for an organization to operate. [3]

The following are the characteristics analyzed to determine institutional racism:

STAFFING PATTERN refers to the number of jobs or employees that carry out the activities and their racial distribution within the association. [4] There is an inverse relationship between staffing and membership. A lack of black members tends to result in a lack of black staff.

ROLE AND FUNCTION refers to the pattern of responsibilities, authority, or positions within the organization. The term "role" is often ambiguous. To avoid confusion, the word "function" has been added. Role and function, as one of the multidimensions of an organization, is interrelated with goal, values premise, and program. For example, in describing the different things an organization does, the organization's function is referred to. But, at the same time, the organization's program is alluded to. In many instances the organization's ends and means are often referred to. Along the same axis this could be organizational goal (ends), or tactics, programs, functions (means). Many of these organizational components, in essence, have close approximations as was evidenced in the findings on the various forms of racism. [5]

Mills commented that in analyzing organizations, it is helpful to think of positions or roles rather than individuals in them. He wrote, "an organization is a system of roles graded by authority." [6]

ORGANIZATION VALUES OR "WORLD VIEW" refers to the basis or premises upon which the organization carries out its mission. Members of the organization are socialized to accept the norms and values of the organization. The basic concept as used here, embraces more than ideology or opinions in the professional organization. It includes the characteristic ways in which the organization approaches the world about them—"how they see it, feel about it, describe it, and act toward it." This thinking (ideology), speaking (official stance), acting (program), is a "world view" which reflects a value system that is identified with the role and function, and goals specifically and tends to permeate all the other organizational patterns in an association. Organizations are conditioned by cultural values and in turn their role is identified by the values of society. [7]

MEMBERSHIP PATTERN refers to one of the main characteristics of an organization. This is a definable group interacting in fairly regularized patterns. Members have become one of the principal units of an organization. They provide much of the basis for social theory in organizations because of their integral relationship with the other components in the organization. [8] Membership pattern, as a form of racism, is related to the categories of membership, scholarship and awards, and recruitment. The latter two provide solutions for increasing black representation in the organization.

GOALS refers to the prescribed ends or desired state of affairs which an organization attempts to realize. The goal or objective provides the purpose toward which the organization's decisions and activities are directed. As terms, goals, value premise or "world view," and role and function parallel the same axis. [9]

PROGRAM ACTIVITY refers to the activities or work of the organization. In analyzing the components of white professional organizations, there is a relationship between program activity and role and function of the organization. The program reflects the purpose for which the organization was set up.

PUBLICATIONS refers to the written materials and various types of communication media used by an association. These include periodicals such as newsletters, articles, journals, and books. As used in this classification scheme, both the methods of communication and the content material are embodied in the term. Publications could be part of a program, but the latter is dealt with separately for purposes of analysis.

CONFERENCES refers to a formal meeting of a number of people for consultation or discussion. It is both an educational opportunity and process used in imparting knowledge but numerous other objectives can be achieved. [10] "Conferences," as an indicator of racism, is related to program activity, membership, and education and training.

SCHOLARSHIPS, AWARDS AND GRANTS refers to

those prizes, gifts, and aids which are provided for members or nonmembers. As a form of racism, scholarships and awards are related to membership, education and training, program activity, and recruitment. Scholarships can expand the membership base, provide for more training and education so that blacks get the academic requirements for acceptance into the profession and in the association. Scholarships and awards are related to program activity, since this might be a major area of emphasis for the association.

RECRUITMENT refers to the process of securing or attracting candidates for membership in the association, staff, or in the profession. Recruitment is related to membership, staffing, and program activity.

EDUCATION AND TRAINING refers to the formal process whereby accredited schools and credentials, conferences, and other educational media provide knowledge, standards, and skills for training in social work and health. [11]

FUNDING SOURCE refers to the means by which an association receives financial support for operations. The kinds of financial resources available to an organization are dependent upon the kinds of goals and programs which it conducts.

EVALUATION OF PROGRAMS refers to the criteria by which an organization determines whether or not its goals are achieved. Evaluation is related to goals and staffing. If the goals are racist as well as the persons assessing the programs, then the final assessment rejects racial overtones.

OFFICIAL POSITION ON SOCIAL ISSUES refers to the stance regarding an issue of importance to blacks or other minority groups, which is sanctioned or authorized by the association.

COALITION AND ALLIANCE refers to the organization's use of merger or alliance with special interest groups to deal with the problems facing minority groups. [12]

NOTES

1. Amitai Etzioni, *Modern Organizations*, (Englewood Cliffs, New Jersey: Prentice-Hall, Inc., 1964).

2. Bronislaw Malinowski, *A Scientific Theory of Culture and Other Essays*, (Chapel Hill: University of North Carolina Press, 1944), p. 52.

3. Amitai Etzioni, "Two Approaches to Organizational Analysis: A Critique and a Suggestion." *Administrative Science Quarterly*, (1960), pp. 257-78.

4. Paul C. Bartholomew, *Public Administration*, (Paterson, New Jersey: Littlefield, Adams and Co., 1962), p. 5.

5. Peter M. Blau and Richard Scott, *Formal Organizations: A Comparative Approach*, (San Francisco: Chandler Publishing Co.).

6. Quoted in John Pfiffner and Robert Presthus, *Public Administration*, (New York: Ronald Press Co., 1967), p. 7.

7. James G. March, ed., *Handbook of Organizations*, (Chicago: Rand McNally and Co., 1965). Herbert A. Simon, *Administration Behavior*, (New York: Free Press, 1966), pp. 199-200.

8. Pfiffner and Presthus, *ibid.*, p. 8.

9. Etzioni, *Modern Organizations, ibid.*, p. 20.

10. Louis Lowry, *Training Manual for Human Service*, (New York: Harper and Row, 1962).

11. O. Glenn Stahl, *Public Personnel Administration*, (New York: Harper and Row, 1962), pp. 295-96.

12. John Foreg, "Chicanos and Coalitions as a Force for Change," *Social Casework*, LII (May 1971), pp. 269-73.

4 | Black Social Workers' Perceptions of Institutional Racism

THE FINDINGS OF THE PERCEPTIONS of the black leaders regarding racism in the national white associations are reported in two categories: total percent of perceptions of racism among subjects; and the rank order of the specific pattern of racism.

The percentage is based on the total number of subjects who identified a specific form of racism. The percentage of subjects is based on the total number of subjects. For an example: Official Position has 93 percent of social workers responding which means that 14 of the 15 subjects responded to this manifestation of racism.

In analyzing forms of racism as perceived by the social work leaders, several forms were more frequently perceived than others. The frequency distribution is reported and then ranked. The forms are manifested in the following rank order of frequency: (1) Staffing, (2) Conferences; Publications, (3) Program Activity, (4) Membership; Official Position on Social Issues; Role and Function, (5) Goals, (6) Organizational Values or "World View," (7) Coalitions and Alliances; Funding Source, (8) Education and Training, (9) Evaluation of Programs; Recruitment, (10) Scholarships, Awards and Grants. They will be dealt with in that sequence here.

Staffing. Among the subjects, about 93 percent perceived the Staffing Patterns among white, established, professional associations as racist.

To illustrate this frequent manifestation of racism, one respondent observed:

> The tendency of these organizations is to select staff largely because they are white; to indicate that they have minority group involvement without involving the minority groups represented by such staff in the selection of such people. These people tend to have roles that are designed to sharpen the nature of the relationship between the white institutions and the minority group. Usually a special effort is made to bring in minority group members as a way of preventing external criticism of the organizations. Such members are not usually brought in upon the same criteria as other members. These members serve some speical institutional function as opposed to staff line function. . . . That is, the black guy becomes the expert on black people, the Chicano becomes expert on all Chicano people. No one becomes the expert on all white people.

> . . .The role and function of the minority group member in such organizations is usually not very circumscribed, as minority group people in such organizations find themselves on a lot of committees making minority group input and their total role is making input. Very seldom do they have decision-making responsibilities. If they do have decision-making responsibility, all kinds of constraints are put on them. In fact, there is a direct relationship between a minority group person in power and the constraints upon him.

Staffing, as a form of racism, was the most frequently perceived form of racism. There appeared to be a definite relationship between Staffing and Membership as perceived categories of racism. Obviously, if blacks are excluded from membership and are alienated in the organization, then it would follow that they are not participants in carrying out the activities, including the decision-making process, in the organization.

The fact that the black social workers would perceive the white association's Staffing Pattern as racist was in keeping with the thrust of black militancy which called for a redistribution of some of the benefits and services, such as jobs, as well as some of the redistribution of the decision-making power.

Conferences. Of the total number of subjects, 87 percent perceived Conferences as a manifestation of racism in white, professional organizations. In regards to the racist pattern in Conferences, one interviewee observed:

> Many of the conferences have been very irrelevant; the kinds of people who are involved in planning the kinds of things that they would hope to accomplish through the conference suggests racism. The conference planners call upon the same, stale, white people to chair the meetings, which is usually a very non-dynamic, therapeutic, self-serving conference. The objectives were to keep membership up, probably, rather than achieve broader goals and objectives.

Another respondent observed, in relation to conferences, that

> nothing on behalf of blacks has taken place at conferences. . . . They have not involved the con-

ferees, but only have the conference to be told the issue. Only recently are there a growing number of black people at conferences, largely because the white control agencies located in black communities cannot function without black staff and because many of the white agencies, you know, are outside the black community. ,... The major thrust of the conference is still white, although black and Puerto Rican workshops are set up to appease these people... They don't think about integrating the major thrust.

Another interviewee said:

Conferences are talk-fests. White and black conferences have not much to say...Some blacks got sick of rhetoric and decided that if we were not going to analyze situations and come up with some kind of meaningful action which would then establish more effective delivery systems, they did not want to take part in any more conferences.

One respondent observed that the conferences among white, established organizations were not geared toward action for relieving the black suffering:

...They were designed for intellectualizing the problems and not trying to implement or deal with the nitty-gritty plan of action.

One interviewee, in observing the small representation of blacks at conferences, said:

Attendance is based upon who gets selected from the agency, and this reflects the staffing pattern... More often, the persons who attend are the top level staff, most of whom are white. So, there are few blacks at conferences . . . Agency selection is based on how long you have been there; what your position is; all of that business—and if top positions are criteria, then black people aren't at that level. They are automatically left out.

Conferences represented the second most frequently perceived form of racism. There appears to be some overlap between the categories of Conferences, Program Activity, Publications, and Education and Training. Conferences are often one of the forms of program, and a means of education for professional associations. In many instances, the publications are based on proceedings and reports of conferences. Consequently, the high perception of conferences as a racist indicator may be connected with this overlap. Conferences, too, became one of the places for some of the most active demonstrations of protest and offered much visibility for direct confrontation of issues. The racist patterns in conferences shown by the lack of black participants and content related to black interests, provided a major focus which could be readily perceived by the social workers.

Publications. Of the total number of subjects, a significant number, 87 percent, perceived Publications as a form of racism in the organization. Among the subjects this was one of the most frequently cited examples of racism. Because of the large percentage of perceptions, several are offered to illustrate how this pattern reveals itself.

In recognizing the various racist patterns among the NASW publications, one interviewee cited:

The editorial committee, to my knowledge, has never had anybody on it, black or white, who has legitimately related to interests of the black community. . . During an eight-year period, I have submitted about five articles, but all were rejected by NASW. Yet, many of the articles were published by many other publications. There were many requests for many of my unpublished articles. They have stayed away from my stuff because what I have to say questions their basic existence. Whenever an article that was "too radical" was published, the NASW would go out and recruit someone to write an alternate article.

Another interviewee observed:

. . . As a national publication they do not deal with black liberation, even though my stuff, which was rejected, may not have been good enough for their publication. I think racism is operating within that publication structure—look at all the Jewish names on the Editorial Board. Those persons who tend to review the anonymous material cannot deal with material written from a black perspective. They are not even involved in black liberation.

In citing his perception of racism in publications, the following respondent said:

It is only recently that most of the established social work organizations with publications discovered that black people could write. This had to come after blacks started to write in their own journals. . . Why? Purely competitive so that they could continue to sell social welfare periodicals to both blacks and whites who were interested in blacks.

To illustrate his perception, another respondent commented:

> Very few articles were accepted from blacks, although blacks were saying much more than many of the articles that were being accepted. They had their own standards based on their own criteria, their own treadmill, and this is for the most part the thing. . . Some of them are just beginning to put out special editions on blacks in an effort to counteract. They can perceive their own racism and react. . . This shows the kind of racism that exists and the impact a new black group can have!

Another interviewee observed:

> Whose writings get published are very much reflected by who the conference speakers are. The publications are only a reflection of the web of racism. Conferences, publications, hotel accommodations, services, and consultants are all a part of it. . . Everything is a spin off. . . And the publications are tied up because the publications come from the speakers and if it's a public racist thing to get speakers, then the publication is reflecting their attitudes. . .

Among the forms of racism, Publications was among the upper half of the patterns. Publications ranked second along with Conferences among the perceptions, showing a close relationship to Programs and Conferences. It is one of the most visible, tangible areas of activity in professional associations, and would be easily perceived by the young social workers as an obvious area for protest.

Program Activity. Of the total number of subjects interviewed, 80 percent perceived Program Activity as a racist pattern in established, white organizations. Illustrative of the racism among program activities was one leader's comment on NASW:

> Welfare reform, as it relates to black people and poor people in this country, was not confronted by the NASW in a viable manner. . . There would not have been need for the National Welfare Rights Organization if they had addressed themselves to this problem.

Another interviewee, in noting the white association's programs which lack accountability to the black community, said:

> Although they talk about their humanity for all people, the associations do not touch the kinds of things they could, probably because of the context of where they are, living in a community that is primarily white. There are many things that develop within the community that they do not touch, which should be addressed to.

Program Activity, was among the third most frequently perceived form of racism.

Membership. Of the total number of subjects, 73 percent perceived the Membership Policy as a racist variable in the established white organization. One leader said that

> the membership pattern in NASW does not reflect black participation. . . They have been hesitant even to have associates for white organizations, which is not full membership. They (blacks) should

not come in as associates, but as a viable force in terms of making changes within that structure... They should be interested in trying to bring into the mainstream the paraprofessional group, to make them useful in terms of social reform for black people.

Another interviewee observed that the NASW membership was racist because of the dues structure and educational criteria:

Both of these criteria have been organized by white people... the people who earn the most money and get the highest pay automatically. This tends to cut off a lot of people who are, in fact, doing the same service in black communities.

Another interviewee perceived the NASW membership pattern as racist because of its adherence to a repressive educational system:

The restrictions are: fewer blacks with high school academic diplomas; fewer blacks graduating from college; fewer blacks accepted into schools of social work; schools set up requirements and quotas for blacks. Most blacks went to Howard and Atlanta Universities' Schools of Social Work.

Membership as a racist pattern ranked fourth along with Official Position and Role and Function among the forms of racism. The high order of this category of racism might be expected, based upon the middle-level black professional's own minority group status, even within the context of his professional identity. Within his job and the professional association, his interpersonal relationships are dominated by whites. The paucity of blacks, particularly where there are systematic barriers for excluding the entrance of other members into the profession and the professional association, is attested to by this finding.

Membership pattern as a racist indicator perhaps ranked high, especially since most of the subjects belonged to a national, white, established, professional association. In this instance, the subjects had reference to their actual experience, rather than their perception.

Official Position on Social Issues. Among the total number of subjects, at least 73 percent perceived lack of Official Position on Social Issues as a form of racism in the established white organization. As an example of this form of racism, one interviewee said:

> ... the organizations are in general approving of the current institutional structure of the country, the system which it operates, and are trying to find some way to strengthen their current level of functioning... They are advocates for the system wherein the organization exists simply as socializing instruments to get people to become leaders or to uphold the value of leadership. They are much more interested in perpetuation than in legitimate change or modification.

Another interviewee illustrated his perception of racism as it pertains to the organization's position on social issues in commenting:

> Many things that develop in the community are not touched or addressed by social workers. The whole question of police brutality or due process of law exists. Many black youths are picked up on the street with many of their rights violated. Many of these youths are clients of agencies. The social

workers and agency directors, in many cases, see their clients in trouble or difficulties which are of a racist nature. But they don't deal with it from an organization perspective. . . They should exert some kind of organizational pressure to deal with that kind of stuff. . . I can't see the welfare department getting that much involved . . . The organizations can exert some pressure, but they allow the perpetuation of racism, you know, by *omission*, you see.

Another respondent observed that racism in the association exists because

there has been no dissatisfaction with the profession, or delivery of social services. . . The war on poverty was created without a professional social work organization defending or helping head the program in regards to policy or welfare requirements. . . The issues of hunger, starvation, pollution, or war were not part of the major concerns.

This category of racism was the fourth ranking category. The high frequency may be associated with the fact that the subjects interviewed were primarily activist leaders who recognized, in a period of intense social consciousness, the importance of group pressure, partisan behavior, and organizational power in influencing actions. The fact that the social workers were a younger age group, ranging from 30 to 39, could also be associated with this finding. Protests of the sixties were waged by a militant, black-oriented group like these social workers, who openly challenged the basic foundations and values premises of the established association.

This finding shows that the subjects frequently perceived the established white association's failure to take a stance on social issues. It reinforces the fact that during the black militancy period, official organizational positions were more strongly questioned. Hamilton noted that there was a "politics of spokesmanship," which was common to the period. [1] There were groups who were useful in raising and dramatizing issues; asking that the organization become more democratic and representative; asking that the organization speak out and become visible about some of the concerns.

Based upon this perception of Official Position, some relationship with the perception of Role and Function, and Goals may appear in view of the fact that Official Positions are usually proposed in relation to the Roles, Goals, and Values of the organization and its Coalitions.

Role and Function. Among the subjects, this form of racism was perceived as frequently as Membership and Official Position. Seventy-three percent of the subjects recognized Role and Function as an inherent racist factor in established, white organizations. This is a significant variable, because most of the subjects were saying that the professional organization's mere existence and cause are perpetuating ingrained forms of racism. One leader observed that Role and Function was an indicator of racism because:

> The associations talk about upholding the structure and function of the institution as against questioning the structure and foundation of the institution. Social work tends to build surface institutions rather than help clients to develop policy. The organizations set up programs to give the illusion they're dealing with the problems of blacks. Such organizations as Social Workers for Civil Rights, Association of Black Social Workers, and Social Workers

for Peace have developed because they could not have their needs met within the professional groups like NASW.

The conceptualization of black people as human beings is antithetical to the existence of these organizations. They are based on the fact that they are organized around some way to keep black people in their places.

Another subject observed that the white professional social work organizations function as destructive forces for black people:

Their role can't help but be this when you look at their theory and philosophy, which is to act as a buffer and an organization that will stop change—that will not create change. They advance a value for molding blacks into stereotyped middle-class, white persons without understanding the cultural values of black people.

Among the forms of racism, this category ranked fourth among the various perceptions. The high frequency of this perception is highly associated with other perceptions such as lack of Official Position on Social Issues, Organizational Values or "World View," and Organizational Goals. As an activist, issue-ridden, extremely socially conscious and critical group, it might be expected that they would question the purpose, expectations, and basic tasks of the white associations. To question the officialdom, performance, involvement, and duties of an organization indeed parallels the questioning of its role and function. The subjects were actually dealing with the "heart, core, and the blood" of the organization. This category ranks high, because it tends to follow the mood of the younger, black, militant group. They rejected the legitimacy of the association as being responsive to the interests of blacks.

Goals. Of the total number of subjects, more than half, or 60 percent, perceived the association's Goals as a form of racism. An illustration of the racist goals of white, professional associations was voiced by one of the leaders:

> These organizations have been serving their members and endorsing services to people. This historical support of service-orientation is no longer valid for black people. For black people we need more than services. We need black institutions, economic institutions—banks, control of schools. This is what builds a strong, black community. There is not a social welfare institution in which we have control. Most of the social welfare institutions never talk about becoming independent. This is what NABSW and its local chapters are all about.

> The organizations do not talk about pluralism, but yet are organized to give the illusion they include everybody. The goals do not talk about pluralism. This is a major indicator of racism. If these organizations have pluralistic goals, then why are there Jewish and Catholic social workers outside of NASW. The goals of the professional association are stated in "egalitarian" terms when in fact we live in a society where there are people living among power groups and the fact that they can feel the ethnic component. The analysis of the NASW shows that certain groups have control. . .

Also illustrative of racist goals is the following:

> If you look at the Constitution and By-Laws of most white, social welfare organizations, you will

find that they are only talking about maintaining certain conditions for themselves; maintaining certain professional standards. If they mention client group, it is usually done in the sense of what he has to do to become even associated with the professionals.

As an indicator of racism, Goals ranked fifth in terms of frequency among the categories. The relationship between Values or "World View," Role and Function, and lack of Official Position on Social Issues, might be expected since all these categories are related to the association's goals. These are service-oriented professional associations where goals are related to the internal aspects of the organization.

Organizational Values or "World View." Among the subjects interviewed, 53 percent perceived the predominantly white, established organization's Values framework as an indicator of racism. One interviewee said:

> The white organizations really have an idea of white nationalism. They conceal it behind an ideology of humanitarian, equalitarian concepts. Black professional organizations tend to state affirmatively and positively that they are a black, nationalistic organization. White organizations tend to practice hypocrisy under the title of democracy, whereas the black organizations, in talking about black nationalism, are really practicing Americanism.

Illustrative of organizational "World View" as racist is the following statement:

> Prior to 1967, the concern was essentially one of trying to continue a particular model of operation that was essentially white, middle-class. This sug-

gested then, that there were some people who didn't fit into that. Because of that, they were not worthy of membership. It was a value system that was working for a group of people and agencies. These organizations were not recognizing the worth and dignity of a group and class of people, but giving them what was considered the good life, middle-class, white way.

Among the racist patterns, Organizational Values ranked sixth among the categories. There would appear to be a relationship between the other forms of racism, such as Goals and Role and Function. The social workers, in essence, questioned the major concerns and basic principles of the organizations. Among those nonmembers of white associations, the following reasons for not belonging were given: the organization is irrelevant; or the organization is uninteresting. The majority of this group, however, still raised issues as to what the prescribed method of thought, mode of conduct, and norms were for the white association. The central thrust was a questioning of the values and attitudes which are being upheld by the organization.

Coalition and Alliance. Among the subjects interviewed, 40 percent perceived Coalition and Alliance as manifestations of racism in the white association. In essence, less than half of the respondents had perceived that the established organizations had not used their influence or power to affect institutional policies regarding blacks and other minority groups.

One respondent noted that

many of the predominantly white national associations such as the National Conference on Social

Welfare, speak for the interests of all groups in the country. Whether or not the groups are involved in that process . . . the association has the luxury of dealing with the establishment through lobbying, but without being held accountable by its membership.

Another interviewee said:

The willingness of these organizations to coalesce with organizations who have as a purpose to work for the interest of blacks is nonexistent. I have not seen a single one—NASW, Child Welfare League, Family Service Association, National Conference on Social Welfare, Council on Social Work Education before 1967—take an interest in developing any kind of relationship, and I'm not talking about merger, but a relationship with an existing or newly formed organization. This is such an important area, because it's here that these organizations can find some fresh, new ideas, as well as program plans.

Among the categories of racism, Coalition and Alliance ranked seventh. It was inferred that this form might rate more highly during the high level of political activity among black, oppressed people. However, it was not as frequently perceived among the indicators of racism, especially since this was an activist group and the lack of Official Position on Social Issues was high among the perceptions. Both Coalition and Alliance and lack of Official Position are closely related as categories of racism. Official positions by organizations are usually taken in alliance with other similar interest groups. But yet, the social workers did not really perceive the connection between the power and influence brought on by coalitions. It would seem that the social workers' emphasis on lack of official position on social issues was more of a socio-moral orientation rather than a socio-political one. With the political awakening in the black community, a higher perception of group alliance might have been expected, especially among the leaders who were activists and organizers.

Funding Source. Of the total number of subjects, 40 percent perceived the organization's Funding Source as an indicator of racism. One subject observed this form of racism in the following comment:

> You look at some of these organizations and pretty soon some of their programs reflect whoever provides the funds. If the thinking and guidelines of the funding source are racist, then whoever accepts a grant from such an agency has to accept it under those terms . . . and once people start accepting funding of that nature, one of the primary objectives becomes to get funded rather than to carry out whatever it was in the first place. Under such circumstances, the organization is under racist control and has to accept the fact that if money is being given to carry out racist goals—it is here that the cycle of racism continues.

Another subject illustrated this manifestation of racism by citing the following:

> The organizations are able to get money from foundations, who usually achieved their assets off the backs of black people through slavery and exploitation. Foundations tend to give money to "safe" organizations. It is usually the organizations which are involved in letting people who want to,

become part of the society. They don't want to redistribute power and resources.

Among the forms of racism, Funding Sources also ranked seventh. This form of racism was at the low end of the frequency scale. This may be attributed to the remoteness of this subject to young, alienated social workers.

Funding Sources, however, are related to other categories, particularly Role and Function, Goals, Value, Program Activity, and the kinds of Official Position on Social Issues taken by the organization.

Education and Training. Among the subjects, 27 percent perceived the predominantly white association's Education and Training programs as indicators of racism.

One interviewee, in illustrating this racist pattern within professional, national, predominantly white associations, such as the Council on Social Work Education, said that

> they can be indicted because they can influence and shape curriculum content, but yet the kinds of content and experiences which sensitize social workers to the reality of oppressed people in this country are excluded from curriculum. . . . There has not been a systematic attempt on the part of social work education to insure this kind of content would be reflected in curricular offerings. The organizations have done little in the way of educating whites on white racism.

Another respondent noted that

> NASW has done nothing to look at curriculum, to tie up what we're teaching our students with what

is happening in institutions. . . Everything is viewed against the white, middle-class norms, and to be different is to be pathological, and that is not so . . . and we aren't doing anything about it, except perpetuating it.

This category ranked eighth among the perceived forms of racism. Education and Training may be an inherent part of the white professional association's Program Activity, and therefore not as easily perceivable for the subjects.

Evaluation of Programs. Twenty percent of the total subjects perceived Evaluation of Programs in the organizations as racist. One respondent raised these basic questions:

If an organization is service-oriented, how can it possibly know what it is doing unless it has some mechanism for the people to feed into the decision-making process or evaluate effectiveness? How do the members of established organizations rate their performance? . . . Are blacks ever involved in rating or evaluating their performance?

Moving beyond the racism in the evaluative techniques of the white, professional association, one leader perceived the social work profession as manifesting this racist pattern:

. . . But the social work profession is the only profession that I know about who decides what should be done for other people, to do it in the way they think it should be done, and evaluate it themselves to tell whether it has been done well or not.

Evaluation of Programs as a racist indicator ranked ninth, or next to the least perceived forms of racism. It was not readily perceived as a racist indicator.

Recruitment. Among the subjects, 20 percent perceived Recruitment as a racist pattern in established, white organizations. Those who did comment felt the organizations had not been assertive toward bringing blacks and other minorities into their organizations or the profession. White associations do not go outside their circle of friends or their own white world, which usually does not include black people in view of the separate black and white societies in this country. The organizations could have exerted their role in recruitment by setting up scholarship programs to attract minorities to schools of social work and the profession, and by conducting more open recruitment to their executive staff, board, and consulting staffs.

Recruitment also ranked next to last in the categories of racism.

Scholarships, Awards and Grants. Of the total number of subjects, only 13 percent perceived racism in the Scholarships, Awards and Grants plans within the predominantly white associations. This low percentage may be attributable to the fact that most blacks are so remote from actual operations and fringe benefits of the white associations that they do not readily perceive some of the personal benefits that might accrue from the white professional associations.

Among the forms of racism, Scholarships, Awards and Grants programs was the lowest perceived form of racism. This category could be included in the category of Program Activity and therefore was not acutely recognized.

NOTE

1. Charles Hamilton, "Black Militancy," *New York Times Encyclopedic Almanac, 1970,* (New York: Quadrangle Books, 1970), pp. 307-308.

5 | Black Health Administrators' Perceptions of Institutional Racism

PERCEPTIONS OF RACIST PATTERNS in national, white, established, professional associations follow in the rank order of frequency which we found among the black health administrators polled: (1) Conferences, (2) Staffing, (3) Membership, (4) Program Activity, (5) Official Position on Social Issues, (6) Role and Function; Recruitment, (7) Publications, (8) Coalition and Alliance; Evaluation of Programs, (9) Funding Source, and (10) Goals; Organization Values or "World View"; Education and Training; and Scholarships, Awards and Grants.

Conferences. Among the hospital administrators, 80 percent of them perceived Conferences as having racist patterns. As supporting evidence for these observations, the following comments were offered by the health administrators:

> Blacks were sparsely represented in the annual AHA conference prior to 1967. In 1968, Whitney Young, late Executive Director, National Urban League, was the keynote speaker. It was here that NAHSE moved to form its own Black Caucus. Since 1968, "Black Consciousness" has stimulated

more black moderators, panelists, resource people, or other participants among black consumers and professionals at AHA. But it is still tokenism.

My association with AHA conferences goes back to the 40's, when the few black administrators could not be accommodated in the main hotels where the conferences were held. The black administrators would have their own meetings at night at these conferences. . . . We would discuss our common problems: "Consider how we could break down the barriers in AHA and get into the policy-making group so that blacks' hospitals could be improved." . . . AHA gave one or two men token positions on committees. We felt then that integration would be for real and we could disintegrate our organization. We pushed for important positions in AHA, but with little success. Due to the fact that we didn't have anyone in policy-making positions, no gains were made.

Conferences ranked first among the perceptions. This high level of perception may be attributed to the trend for administrators to perceive the most overt and blatant rather than the covert forms of racism. As an older group of professionals, they have been aware of the absence of blacks at meetings and conferences through the years.

Staffing. Among the health administrators, at least 73 percent of them perceived the Staffing pattern as racist. Comments supporting this awareness of racism were made, such as the following:

AHA has been foot dragging, but AHA responded once we (NAHSE) indicated we wanted to get in the mainstream—committees, boards, commissions . . . strategic spots in the organization . . . on the staff, high councils . . . where we can speak out as representing an ethnic group, or otherwise. Just two or three years ago there were no blacks in high administrative positions.

NAHSE has been able to focus its attention on greater participation and involvement in all of the organizations on all levels so that we can have representation rather than tokenism. I think I could see some real progress, but not enough has been done!

Blacks have been at the bottom of the ladder in AHA, ACHA, and even the local level health organizations such as the New York Hospital Association. Blacks are not in policy-making positions. Health is a kind of white man's power base in many instances. Of course, if a black finally lands a position, he must be the "acceptable black," who usually is one who doesn't rock the boat, and rocking the boat is necessary if change is to occur. The "acceptable black" meets the quota and the sad thing about it is that they ride that horse to death. The same black is called on again and again.

Staffing ranked high among the perceptions. It was the second highest category. Some of the same points inferred about Conferences and Membership can also be associated with the perception of Staffing.

Membership. The health administrators—at least 67 percent—perceived Membership pattern as one of the highest categories of racism in established, white professional associations. Some of the national leaders cited that

blacks were excluded from the established white groups. There was no real participation in organizational structure, committee deliberation; no input in policy making. If black input is made, all other areas of racism will disappear.

There is a parallel between the association and the health care delivery system in terms of the systematic pattern of racism as seen in the supply and demand of minority manpower. There is a systematic keeping out and down of black people in the power structure of health care. The fact that all the lower level positions are held by blacks and Puerto Ricans and all the top level people are white is no accident.

Membership was the third highest perceived form of racism among the health administrators. Membership would appear to be high because this is an older group that has been dramatically aware of the absence of blacks in the white association as well as in health administration as a professional discipline. Then, too, this group appears to recognize the more external or tangible evidences of racism, such as Staffing, Conferences, Program Activity, and Scholarships, Awards and Grants.

Program Activity. Among the total number of subjects interviewed, 53 percent perceived Program Activity as an indicator of racism in the white, established professional associations.

Although Program Activity overlaps with the categories of Education and Training and Conferences, one of the subjects illustrated this pattern by this observation:

NAHSE has added a "people consciousness" to the established, white, health organizations, because so many of the programs had no accountability to community people. NAHSE will help to bring about innovations in the delivery of health care and in dealing with the special problems associated with the black community.

Another subject said:

> The white professional associations have been concerned with and endorsed programs which were not designed for the overall problems of health care. Black people have some specific problems. The health problems of the ghetto as compared to the plush suburban areas are quite different.

Program Activity ranked near the middle range (fourth) of all the various perceptions. This ranking could be attributed to the fact that there are a smaller number of responses made by the group as a whole. Consequently, this perception falls at a much higher level of frequency.

Official Position on Social Issues. Of the total subjects, 47 percent perceived the lack of Official Position on Social Issues as a racist indicator in established, white professional associations. The following remarks were made:

> AHA and ACHA have done little in moving toward the affairs of black people. Community control only became an issue for AHA in 1970. The kind of strong position that was necessary on a continuous basis has not been taken by the organizations. The polarization which we know is upon us is just as existent, progressively, in the health care profession now.

> The racism inherent in this category was further illustrated by the National Welfare Rights Organization. They demonstrated at the AHA 1969 meet-

ing and demanded certain rights. These rights shouldn't have to be requested, they should have been part of the health care delivery system.

The organizations with lobbying functions had no cognizance of blacks' needs and representation. The blacks' problem was just ignored, yet the hospitals in the black community were criticized for operating poor hospitals.

The lack of Official Position on Social Issues ranked fifth among the perceptions of racism. The high level of perception may be attributed to the fact that the "black militancy period" was one in which group pressure, speaking out on issues, and advocacy in behalf of special groups were popular. Consequently, the administrators recognized that the black cause and position in the health field had few spokesmen, with the exception of the National Medical Association, the Medical Committee for Human Rights, and OEO, Office of Health Affairs. [1]

As was indicated with the social workers, it might be expected that a closer link with Official Position and Coalition and Alliance might have been made by the health administrators. It is questionable whether these groups really see the dynamics of the political process involved in the advocacy of positions on crucial social issues. The concept of power and use of special interest groups for coalition is beyond simple spokesmanship, rhetoric, or verbal protest.

Role and Function. Among the health administrators, 40 percent perceived Role and Function as a racist pattern in the white, established health professional associations.

This was a low level of perception, reflecting somewhat the less critical and questioning nature of the health administrators. It appears that they did not concern themselves with the basic attitudes, purposes, and services provided by the associations.

Among those who did perceive the Role and Function as a racist pattern, these observations were made:

> The established organizations are protecting their own interests because it is what they have established.

> AHA by no means would openly think they are bigots or have strong prejudices against black people, or against anybody. But when you work within the framework of the establishment where the pattern has been set for a hundred-odd years or more, . . . it's not easy to bother as long as no one makes any noise.

Among the categories of racism, Role and Function ranked sixth, along with Recruitment. Role and Function as an intrinsic element in an organization was in the middle range of racist perceptions among the health administrators.

As an older, less militant group, these subjects did moderately recognize the racial implications ingrained in the Role and Function of the fabric of the white, professional health organizations. This group did not question the status quo all along, but the protest movement helped precipitate overt responses from them.

Recruitment. Among the total number of subjects, 40 percent of them perceived Recruitment as a racist indicator in the white, professional associations. Some of the comments reflecting this pattern observed:

> Large segments of our black population are denied access to the social-educational opportunities

which would allow them to participate in significant numbers as consumers or providers; but the need for health care is highest among the poor and disadvantaged. . . . The professional associations had not addressed themselves to these points by making assertive proposals for the manpower shortage until just recently.

I do not think that any great effort in the past was made to attract blacks into the health field.

Recruitment also ranked sixth among the perceptions. This ranking order may be attributed to the perceptive ability of this group to discern the relationship between Recruitment, Staffing, and Membership. Since Staffing and Membership were high among the perceptions, Recruitment might have been seen as an integral part of these two forms of racism.

Publications. Among the health administrators, 33 percent perceived racism in the Publications category. An example of racism was cited in the following:

With the publication of many of the journals, you really don't see enough publication by blacks. To some degree we might not be publishing ourselves because the hospital situations we are in demand constant action. There are rare instances for sitting down and taking the time to write a great deal, or even to contemplate. So, often, we don't have the adequate resources—financial, staff, library, and features conducive to this type of activity in our hospitals. Blacks are usually in hour-by-hour, crisis situations. We are in hospitals that have never been improved, almost working with nothing.

As a form of racism, Publications ranked seventh, or in the lower range of perceptions. The group did not seem readily aware of racism in Publications on a conscious level. As noted by one of the subjects, writing, reading, and publishing may not be major preoccupations of health administrators as high level managers. This may be attributed to the activist and crisis-oriented nature of their work.

Coalition and Alliance. Among the health administrators, Coalition and Alliance as racist indicators were perceived by 27 percent of them. One of the national leaders made the following statement in documenting his observation:

> AHA has a Lobbying and Legislative Committee which has not pushed member hospitals or consumer groups to enact social programs. They have not advocated any legislation that was favorable to blacks.

Another subject commented:

> For years and years, AHA, AMA, Committee on Accreditation, American College of Surgeons, and ACHA have had paid lobbies in Washington who ignored the black health problem. Blacks may have benefited vicariously by virtue of the fact that total legislation was passed, but their specific problems in operating their institutions were by-passed.

To further illustrate the racism as evidenced by the lack of coalition action among white associations, another subject said:

> Blacks have been excluded from groups like AHA, ACHA when talks with the government or the formulation of bills and acts of Congress are carried out. . . We are not just interested in getting

action for the blacks, we are interested in getting in the mainstream. When you're talking about any program that affects the American people in this country . . . we want to be part of the discussions with HEW, so that we can speak in our own behalf.

Coalition and Alliance ranked eighth among the perceptions. As one of the more external elements in an organization, Coalition was not highly perceived. This reflects, to some degree, the health administrators' lack of perception of the political implications in dealing with health and the black conditions as politico-social issues outside of their own institutional structure. How keenly aware this group is in the area of politics and health is questionable, especially because, as an older group, politics may not have been a part of their education and training; but certainly, the politics issue is not new to them pragmatically as administrators. There appears to be some connection between their middle range perception on Official Position and Coalition as indicators of racism. However, it could be inferred that the higher perception given to Official Position stems from a moral perspective of the racial situation.

Evaluation of Programs. Among the health administrators, 27 percent of them also perceived Evaluation of Programs as a form of racism:

> Professional associations, as members of the health delivery system will have to realize that they can't be the "cook" and also the "judge" on how good the food is. As providers of health care, they will need others to evaluate the quality of health care. Consumers coming in and demanding . . . telling you exactly where they feel the needs are, because the people in the inner city know best where their needs are; they know better than we do.

As a manifestation of racism, Evaluation of Programs was in the lower range of perceptions, ranking eighth.

Funding Source. Among the total number of health administrators, 20 percent perceived Funding Source as a racist pattern. In most instances, when this category was perceived, it had reference to the direct health service organizations rather than to the professional associations. Illustrative of this pattern was the following statement:

> Blacks were not a part of lobbying nor formulating new legislation. Yet, we are often criticized for operating poor hospitals. But, when you find that you do not have the supplementary funds that are necessary to supplement the charges that your lower socio-economic group is able to pay, you need some supplementary funds.

Another respondent noted:

> There have been black hospitals in the AHA, which have a tremendous budget. My hospital pays at least $3,800 per year. Look at the total budget of AHA and the amounts paid by the black hospitals for years. There should have been staff appointments, but there were none. This is a definite sign of racism.

Funding Source was low among the perceptions. In fact, it ranked ninth among the frequency distribution of forms of racism. Health administrators seemingly were not aware of or denied the connections between racism and Funding Source.

Goals. Among the total number of subjects, 7 percent perceived the white health associations' Goals as racist.

Goals were almost imperceptible to this group, since it ranked tenth along with Organizational Values or "World View," Education and Training, and Scholarships, Awards and Grants.

This finding indicated that the health administrators were not a group who questioned the foundation, direction, or premises of the organizations. This might be expected when the characteristics of the health administrators are considered. As an older group, with 80 percent of them having been in the profession for over 10 years, and most of them (80 percent) holding membership in the white, established, professional association, they tended to identify themselves with the organization's explicit objectives, unquestioningly. The health administrators as a traditional, sanctioning group did not raise issues for changing what these associations were trying to achieve. Essentially, they "wanted in," or as one of the subjects said:

> We want to get into the mainstream, in the middle of the action.

As a whole, the health administrators did not question where the mainstream was headed. They entered the profession at a time when they had to be as nearly "white" as possible to be accepted.

The fact that these administrators did not perceive highly the Goals of the white health associations as racist, clearly indicates the total aloofness to getting down to the basic problem of racism even during a time of social protest. It has been apparent that health service institutions and professional bodies were not pursuing the goal of promoting health of the "American" people.

Organizational Values or "World View." Among the total number of health administrators, 7 percent also perceived

Organizational Value or "World View" as an indicator of racism.

Organizational Values and Goals as indicators of racism ranked among the last perceptions of this group.

As an intrinsic element among the organizational components, the Goals or Values on which these established organizations rested went unquestioned by these health administrators. Even though this group felt excluded from the major white groups, they did not raise issues around the Organizational Values base. As an older, moderately dissident group, they tended to deal with more of the obvious and concrete elements of the organization such as Conferences of Membership which exhibited more recognizable and visible patterns of racism. They did, however, question at a higher level the basic Role and Function of the organizations.

Education and Training. Among the subjects, Education and Training was also among the least perceived forms of racism. The health administrators failed to see its relationship to racism in educational and professional associations. In the instance where professional education as a phase of training was mentioned, the following observation was made:

> The whole education process in health administration is evidence of racism. I have statistics which cite that 90 percent of the health administrators in Virginia are graduates of the University of Virginia School of Hospital Administration. The University of Chicago School of Hospital Administration started in 1936, yet has had only six black graduates. This is equivalent to one every five years! This is not because people were not available, but the health care field never opened its doors to management level blacks.

Education also ranked lowest among the perceptions. Even though the AUPHA is one of the main professional education associations, the subjects predominantly chose to criticize the AHA rather than the ACHA. They tended to be closer to problems of practice and operations than to education and training issues. This trend was not expected, particularly since Education and Recruitment have become the main programs of NAHSE.

Scholarships, Awards and Grants. Of the total number of subjects, only 7 percent made mention of Scholarships, Awards and Grants or other benefits as being indicators of racism.

This category of racism, in addition to the latter three forms, ranked last. It was not as highly perceived as Conferences, Publications, Coalitions, and other more external elements in the association. The health administrators, as an older group, perhaps could not readily perceive that they had not been offered many of the scholarships, awards, and other status recognition and symbols given by the white professional associations. However, the older group which was interviewed may not have been involved directly in the NAHSE recruitment program.

NOTE

1. Herbert M. Morais, "Medicine and Health," *In Black America, 1968: The Year of Awakening,* ed. by Patricia W. Romero, (Washington, D.C.: Association for Study of Negro Life and History, 1969), p. 365.

6 | Comparative Perceptions
of Institutional Racism

THE CENTRAL FOCUS OF THIS STUDY is concerned with a comparative analysis of the perceptions of institutional racism in established, white, professional associations among social workers and health administrators. The research findings suggest some generalizations which we shall outline.

The comparative approach as a methodology in descriptive research entails some hazards, according to Blau and Scott. [1] It is observed that generalizations based on uncontrollable situations entail some risks. As in the case of this study, where an observer actually conducted field interviews with members of only two organizations (of one of which he was a member himself), the validity of the generalizations could be questioned. However, the primary leadership of both groups is compared. Despite the risks in the approach, it is felt that a comparison of the differences and similarities in two groups' perceptual levels of institutional racism can be both useful and revealing. Hopefully, it will provide some insights into the external and internal aspects of racism in professional associations. All of the perceptions have significant relevance to the socio-political context of today's organizational life. Comparisons of forms of racism, as perceived by the leaders, are presented in the order of their frequency of occurrence among the social workers. In our discussions we are using the health administrators as the comparison group. Each group is discussed in relation to the fifteen indicators of racism (see Tables 12, 13, and 14).

Staffing. Both social workers and health administrators perceived Staffing as a high-level indicator of racism. (For the social workers, there was a 93 percent return on the responses, as against 73 percent for the health administra-

Table 12

COMPARATIVE PERCEPTIONS OF INSTITUTIONAL RACISM
BY BLACK SOCIAL WORKERS AND
HEALTH ADMINISTRATORS

Perceptions	Social Workers		Health Administrators	
	Rank	*Percent**	*Rank*	*Percent**
Staffing	1	93	2	73
Conferences	2	87	1	80
Publications	2	87	7	33
Program Activity	3	80	4	53
Membership	4	73	3	67
Official Position	4	73	5	47
Role and Function	4	73	6	40
Organization Goals	5	60	10	7
Organization Values	6	53	10	7
Coalition	7	40	8	27
Funding Source	7	40	9	20
Education and Training	8	27	10	7
Evaluation	9	20	8	27
Recruitment	9	20	6	40
Scholarships and Awards	10	13	10	7

*Percentage is based on the total number of subjects who responded to a specific form of racism.

Table 13

COMMON PERCEPTIONS AMONG SOCIAL WORKERS
OF INSTITUTIONAL RACISM

Racism Indicators	Rank	Percent
Conferences	2	87
Publications	2	87
Membership	4	73
Official Position	4	73
Role and Function	4	73
Coalition and Alliance	7	40
Funding Source	7	40
Evaluation	9	20
Recruitment	9	20

tors.) Staffing ranked number 1 and 2 among the perceptions for the respective groups. The fact that Staffing was high among the perceptions is attributed to some of the same factors which are mentioned in Membership. The groups obviously have seen over the years the absence of minority group persons in various staff positions, such as line staff, executive staff, boards or commitees (policy-making), and consultants.

Table 14

COMMON PERCEPTIONS AMONG HEALTH ADMINISTRATORS
OF INSTITUTIONAL RACISM

Racism Indicators	Rank	Percent
Role and Function	6	40
Recuitment	6	40
Coalition and Alliance	8	27
Evaluation	8	27
Goals	10	7
Values or "World View"	10	7
Education and Training	10	7
Scholarships and Awards	10	7

Conferences. The perception of Conferences as a form of racism was another highly perceived form of racism for both social workers and health administrators. Social workers perceived it in 87 percent of the responses, while health administrators perceived it in 80 percent. Conferences was the number 1 perception for the health administrators and number 2 for the social workers. The high perception is predictable because Conferences represents one of those visible forms of racism, and particularly because it was the major focal point of protest in the late sixties. The collective pressure and organizing became a trend with the increased emphasis on "blackness." The various white, national, professional conferences where black caucuses were held dramatically illustrated racism among the Conferences.

Publications. Among the two groups, Publications appeared in extreme ranges of the perceptions of racism. A higher percentage (87 percent) of the responses was made by the social workers than by the health administrators (33 percent).

The ranking order for Publications was second and seventh, respectively, for the social workers and health administrators. As practitioners, leaders and activists, the social workers were more prone to engage in writing and were knowledgeable about the various facets of the publication process. This was also attributable to the fact that many of the social workers were recent graduates whose education relied heavily on written materials.

Although health administrators were activist, they were less given to writing and were less sophisticated concerning the various facets of the publication process. Were they a group of faculty members in schools of hospital administration, their response might have been higher. The academician is more prone to engage in the activities associated with publication such as writing, research, and participation on editorial boards.

Program Activity. As a form of racism, Program Activity was high in the perceptions for both groups. For the social workers, 80 percent of the subjects perceived this area as compared with 53 percent of the health administrators.

The ranking order was third for social workers and fourth for health administrators. Obviously, both groups rate Program Activity high among the perceptions. Among the variables associated with this is the fact that little of the white organization's activities or work was directly related to the black experience. As mentioned earlier, the high frequency of this perception for the health administrators must be seen also in the context of the smaller number of forms which they could identify as types of Program Activity.

Membership. Among the groups of leaders, Membership was highly perceived as a form of racism. Seventy-three percent of the social workers and 67 percent of the health administrators perceived this overt pattern of racism. The former ranked Membership as the number 4 form of racism and the latter rated it as number 3 among the manifestations of racism.

This high-level perception of Membership is related to the fact that both groups of black professionals were keenly aware of the paucity or complete absence of minority group members, and related as well to their self-interest and to the political motivation in the white associations. They were also aware that there are various membership criteria such as education, accreditation standards, superficial interpersonal relations between black and white professionals, dues, as well as poor public relations activities which fail to attract larger numbers of minority persons.

The high perception of Membership as a racist indicator is probably associated with the intense feelings of alienation that both groups of black professionals have experienced in the white professional associations. They may have been members of, but not really members *in* these associations. Consequently, this phenomenon may have led to the form of protest which fostered pro-black and all-black national organizations. [2]

Official Position on Social Issues. Among both groups of subjects, the social workers had the highest percentage, 73 percent, of perception of the lack of Official Position on Social Issues. The health administrators had a lower perception, 47 percent of their members recognizing this form of racism.

The lack of Official Position ranked number 4 in the frequency distribution for social workers, whereas it was number 5 for the health administrators, both groups ranking it high. The level is probably attributable to the fact that the late sixties fostered a climate in which protest and advocacy of social concerns were popular. [3] Individuals and organizations could more openly express their views and positions in a time of extreme social consciousness and upheaval.

Role and Function. There was a similarity in the perception of Role and Function among the social workers and health administrators. It was high among the perceptions of social workers (73 percent), ranking fourth. The social workers appeared to be a more perceptive group when it came to questioning the *basic* purposes and role of the established, white associations.

For the health administrators, Role and Function was

among the moderately perceived categories of racism. Only 40 percent perceived this category; the ranking order was number 6, as was Recruitment. The health administrators, especially as an older group of leaders, appeared to perceive less frequently the health associations' basic foundations and philosophies as racist, although these associations were not responsive to the needs and aspirations of either black professionals or black consumers. It could also be that this group was more concerned with the hard, day-to-day work of organizing blacks to gain some leverage through more positions and more recruits to the program. This finding may have some relevancy to the fact that there are those whose protest consists of articulating issues and there are those whose protest focuses on negotiations.

Goals. Among the two groups, Goals was higher among the perceptions of social workers than health administrators. Sixty percent of the social workers perceived and ranked Goals as the fifth most frequent manifestation of racism.

The health administrators almost did not perceive Goals as a racist indicator: only 7 percent perceived this specific form, ranking it near the bottom. While the age and political differences are factors, perhaps the health administrators' analytical ability in relation to racist indicators in organizations was difficult to verbalize. Goals, as a concept, is also not as visibly evident to this group. The subjects, on various occasions, spoke of racism in relation to the direct service organization rather than to the professional association toward whose Goals they voiced no exception. Although certain objectives have been mandated by the ACHA, such as elevating standards of competence in hospital administration, standards of education and training for hospital administraters, none of the goals was challenged in relation to their implications for blacks. [4] The AHA Code of Ethics regarding hospital ethics, principles of conduct for hospital administration, nor the administrative principles were questioned. [5]

Organization Values. This was held to be one of the substantive elements which could indicate racism. There was a greater percentage of perception of Values among social workers than health administrators. At least 53 percent of the social workers ranked Values at level 6. Seven percent of the health administrators ranked Values in the lowest category of racism.

Coalition and Alliance. This investigation inferred that, depending upon the degree to which an established, white organization makes use of Coalition and Alliance (political environment) in behalf of black special interest groups, this could serve as an indicator of racism in the organization.

Coalition and Alliance was perceived at a rather low level by both social workers and health administrators: 40 percent for the social workers; 27 percent for the health administrators. A ranking order of 7 was given to Coalition and Alliance among the social workers, while it ranked 8 with the health administrators.

A higher frequency might have been expected particularly since both groups present an increasing emphasis on socio-political awareness in the black community. Perhaps this finding supports the observation that the real thrust of the "new spirit" of revolutionary militancy had its greatest relevance for the militant black youth. Contemporary black militancy was adopted in varying degrees by different groups and individuals. But the one common characteristic of all groups was their effort to gain a measure of safety, power, and dignity. This was apparent even among middle-level, black professionals. [6]

Funding Source. Funding Source was also in the second half of the perception for both groups. The low percentage (20 percent) and ninth rank of the responses from health administrators indicate that not much significance was attached to Funding Source as a racist indicator. Funding was in the seventh position for social workers (40 percent).

The low ranking order may indicate that these groups have been rather remote from the Funding Source of these white associations, obscuring the connections between Funding Source and racism. Even the allocation of funds (budgeting) as an internal aspect of the operation and management of the organization is not readily recognized as an index to racism. What money is spent for what programs and what groups benefit or receive services—as indicators of who reaps the benefits from an association— were subtleties to this group.

Education and Training. Both social workers and health administrators perceived this as one of the lowest ranking categories—eighth for the social workers (27 percent), and tenth for the hospital administrators (7 percent). In view of the linkage of Education and Training with the also low-ranking categories of Scholarships, Awards and Grants, and Recruitment, the low perceptual level might be anticipated.

The fact that Education and Training was lower among the perceptions of health administrators may be attributed to their preoccupation with the practice aspects rather than the Education and Training aspects of their profession. A higher level might have been expected from the social workers, even though leaders and "doers," but many of them were more recent professional graduates. They had questioned curriculum content and minority representation on the faculty and student body. Many had charged the professional associations with neglect of the justified demands of the minorities, and challenged them to develop realistic responses. [7]

Evaluation of Programs. Twenty percent of the social workers had perceived this specific form of racism, while even more of the health administrators (27 percent) had perceived it. The ranking order for health administrators was also higher (eighth) than it was for social workers (ninth).

In examining an organization for racist indicators, one may not readily discern the Evaluation aspect. In fact, this is often overlooked amidst involvement in the day-to-day administrative operations. The manner in which the associations critically assessed their performance did not frequently occur to social workers or health administrators as an indicator of institutional racism.

Recruitment. The Recruitment pattern among white, established professional associations was low among the perceptions of both groups—lowest for social workers; low, too, for health administrators, but succeeded by other covert and overt forms of racism. Recruitment shared its sixth ranking position with Role and Function among the health administrators. Among social workers, its rank was shared with Evaluation of Programs at the ninth position. A 20 percent response was made by social workers, and the significant rate of 40 percent, by health administrators.

Although the health administrators' Recruitment program was a major activity (and will be discussed in Chapter 8), it could be inferred that this category should have been even more frequently perceived. But the group interviewed on the whole was not comprised of those directly involved in Recruitment. Nevertheless, this does reflect the degree of consensus or knowledge about program among a broader base of the membership.

One would expect the social workers to perceive Recruitment as a racist indicator more frequently than they did, since many were recent graduates and had advocated more minority admissions to schools of social work and to the profession. In view of Recruitment's relationship to other forms of racism such as Staffing, Membership, Scholarships, Awards and Grants, and Education and Training, more opinions on it might have been expressed.

Scholarships, Awards and Grants. As an indicator of racism, this category was not highly perceived by either the social workers or the health administrators. Only 13 percent of the social workers responded to this form of racism, and it was ranked at the bottom. Among the health administrators, it was also low, along with Goals, Organization Values or "World View," and Education and Training. Some 7 percent of them responded to this specific form of racism, and ranked it tenth along with the other categories.

Of special interest is the fact that health administrators as an older, educated group perceived this category at a similar level to the younger social workers. The latter group might have been expected to be more likely to relate racism to Scholarships, Awards and Grants, since they were more recently graduates of professional schools. Yet the health administrators perceived this manifestation of racism almost as keenly. It should be borne in mind, however, that the health administrators have conducted a more active recruitment program, especially because black health administrators are so rare. They have recognized that the scholarship assistance and awards programs have not been accessible to black candidates, despite the fact that these kinds of support and special services are needed to attract more blacks into health administration.

WHY THE DIFFERENCES IN PERCEPTIONS?

Major Differences in Perceptions. Essentially, the findings reveal that social workers were more perceptive than health administrators about racist patterns in white, professional organizations. Both groups perceived primarily the overt forms of racism, with the exception of the social workers' higher perception of such covert forms as Role and Function, Goals, and Publications. In general, the social workers perceived both covert and overt forms of racism, and there was a greater percentage of response by them on each specific form of racism.

In general, the health administrators perceived only the most obvious or overt forms of racism, with the exception of Role and Function. Moreover, the health administrators made almost no recognition of the established, white associations' Goals or Organization Values. This raises serious questions as to whether this group is introducing substantial, innovative challenges to established professional associations, and whether or not this group is dealing with structural change in developing new organizations. If their perceptions of white institutions have not been critical, then they must become aware of how those institutions function, or, said in another way, they must come to understand these intrinsic, internal and covert aspects of essentially racist institutions.

Why should there be such significant differences in the perceptions of social workers and health administrators? Among the influential factors are age, economic status, social climate, education, personality types, and the nature of the two professions—with all of which we shall deal.

Differences in Age, Economic Status. While the age differential is an obvious factor, it cannot be considered apart from its relationship to the educational experiences, the black militancy period, and the types of professions involved. An older group, the health administrators revealed a greater degree of moderation in their dissidence. They had been employed longer and received higher salaries; thus they had a greater number of personal assets based on their status, prestige and income.

Because of their own status quo, traditionally oriented situation, health administrators viewed the mood of black militancy quite differently. They could not accommodate this militancy within the context of their professional status, their assimilation of the white frame of reference, and their relative conservatism. They also were accustomed to making few open demands upon the established associations. Although alienated, too, the health administrators had managed to identify their interests with those of the white associations.

By contrast, in this period of social upheaval, the younger, black social workers were the first black professionals to organize nationally to deal with the racist social welfare structure. [8] As a younger group, with fewer vested interests and less economically secure, social workers tended to be somewhat more radical in their perceptions. They perceived the Official Position, Goals, Organization Values, and Role and Function as forms of racism in the established, white organizations. Here, the group was taking on the more critical, analytical role in protest. The current wave of black activist militancy and the creation of black institutions contributed to many of these perceptions.

It could be inferred that the increasing political awareness in the black community would especially affect such perceptions as these. As a younger group, less tied to the establishment and having newly entered the profession, their minds were opened by the political environment which emphasized power blocs, the removal of oppression, the freedom and liberation theme, and representative democracy. Thus, this group identified with the efforts to deal with the inequalities in the organization and the need to change these.

These social workers, however, tended to contraindicate an earlier study's proposition that social workers of high occupational status are conservative in their conceptions of strategies for change in the profession. [9] This study must be questioned because it did not consider the social climate of the black social workers, nor was it a representative sample of radical social workers. The black group of social workers in this study was not conservative but really dealt with some of the more incisive, intrinsic elements of an organization.

Differences in Education. The health administrators were educated in southern black colleges. During their professional career, many of their efforts involved fighting racial barriers to gain admittance to the American Hospital Association or American College of Hospital Administration. Much of their professional activity was devoted to eliminating internal discrimination in the white, professional health associations. Consequently, their perception of institutional racism contrasts strongly with the social workers'.

The majority of the social workers were educated in northern, white universities. Their professional careers indicated that they did not have to encounter as many racial barriers to entering many of the white, professional, social welfare organizations. Not having been ego-involved in this process, they could readily protest about the goals, values, purposes, and actions of the associations which were not compatible with their own.

Differences in Personality Types. Various behavioral scientists have outlined the effects of different personality types on bureaucratic structure. [10] Because the social structure involves certain defined patterns and norms, certain kinds of personality configurations adapt to the roles and expectations of the organizational context.

Associations have been made between certain personality types and occupational categories. The relationship between values and the kind of work one undertakes was studied by Rosenberg, Nosow, and others. [11] In a study of occupational choice and "faith in people," teaching and science ranked at the top. "Self-interested" vocations such as business, finance, and public relations ranked at the bottom. The latter occupations were chosen by people with high mobility drives and low faith in people. The aggressive personality type who respects only the powerful and successful was found to be more self-confident and manipulative. He chose the "organizing-administrative occupations." The detached type who craved his own independence chose fields such as art, architecture, and natural science.

These different values place people for different occupational backgrounds in strained relations. For example, professors and administrators each define situations and motivation because of their different "self system." Professors are often "people-oriented" and administrators are usually and necessarily concerned with control, techniques, and financial considerations. [12]

An examination of some of the personality dimensions among health administrators and social workers offers some explanation for the differences in their perceptions of institutional racism.

Health administrators, in general, are a conforming and orderly type. Their rational, logical traits are a prerequisite to effective bureaucracy.

The social workers are verbal, aggressive, and socially aware. Their work is people-oriented rather than custodial, institutional-maintenance oriented. Because social workers are more involved with people, they tend to have a high level of awareness and sensitivity to Social Issues, Programs, Goals, and Values.

Differences in the Nature of the Professions. The type of jobs performed by health administrators and social workers is another factor contributing to the differences in perceptions of institutional racism.

Health administration has been a more focused profession. It is somewhat younger as a profession and an educational process than social work. [13] Traditionally, the profession has had an institutional focus, and only recently do we see the trend toward a broader perspective for its participation and role. This essentially has led hospital administration to change its professional identity from one of specialization to generalization—health care administration, or medical administration, or administrative medicine rather than simply hospital administration. [14]

Hospital administration, in a sense, has been predicated on a more local and institutional boundary when the role orientation is observed. [15] The comparisons of roles between social workers and health administrators could be associated with Gouldner's model of "locals" and "cosmopolitans." [16]

The health administrators, as "locals," behave somewhat more like organizational men with a strong orientation to the values and expectations of the institution. Consequently, they perceived little covert racism in the white, health association. These individuals still "wanted in" the white association. Perhaps the prestige, status, and acceptance were still important to them. They are a rational, loyal group who could justify the white association's policies and constraints in view of their lack of perceptions of racism. The majority of the health administrators had been in the profession ten or more years and were perhaps somewhat more socialized to its culture, although they are outsiders to the total profession.

From an occupational point of view, the perceptions made by the social workers correspond closely with the nature of the social work profession. Pervasive perceptions are characteristic of that profession which in some way must act as the "social conscience" to the society. Social work as a marginal profession, observed Rapport,

> seems to be outside the mainstream of society. The profession symbolically serves as an ever present reminder of society's failures and lacks in its social and moral responsibilities. This particular role of the profession, as has been observed, gives it the attribute of a minority group in society. It has been noted that social workers ideologically tend to identify with problems and needs of economically and socially disadvantaged groups which they largely serve. . . In addition, its social views tend to alienate social workers as individuals from their own class and intimates. . . Thus, as a profession in society, social workers hold a position of marginality. [17]

With this kind of mission, social workers can't help but be sensitized to the inequities and discriminations in established, white professional associations.

Thus, one might expect this broader range of perceptions among social workers. In addition to its preoccupation as a "social conscience" for the society, social work requires a pervasive, broader range of knowledge, values, and skills because of its interdisciplinary nature and demands for problem-solving.

Here again, Gouldner's model on role set provides an interesting comparison for professional role-orientation between social workers and health administrators. The social workers are comparable to the "cosmopolitans." In addition, the social workers' broader perspective and approaches to the nature of their jobs increase this cosmopolitan outlook. The group was less identified with the white organization's Goals, Values, and "World View." As a group, the social workers are not as conservative about stability and continuity of the established, white, professional organization.

General Conclusions. Based on these findings and interpretations of black perceptions of institutional racism among social workers and health administrators, the following generalizations are made:

1. Black professionals tend to perceive overt forms of racism. Institutional racism as a concept is subtle and difficult to discern.

2. Black professionals, in general, do not question the covert, more ingrained forms of racism in the white professional organizations. The covert forms of racism are often the more significant, intrinsic elements such as Standards, Goals, Values, and Role and Function of the associations. This finding raises the issue as to whether these groups have raised hard questions which challenge long-standing values, beliefs, and institutions. The issue is whether these newly emerged black professional groups are another form of structural change. They may not raise the questions in relation to the white associations, but may inculcate new principles in the separate organizations.

3. Black professional groups do perceive a political orientation of the white, established, professional associations' use or non-use of Coalitions and Alliances as a means for fostering the interests of blacks.

4. Younger, black professionals (under thirty-five) and newcomers to the profession have expressed more militant, radical dissidence.

5. Younger, black professionals who are less assimilated socially and economically, made the most substantive and challenging perceptions of institutional racism in regards to Values, Goals, Role and Function of white associations.

NOTES

1. Peter M. Blau and W. Richard Scott, *Formal Organizations: A Comparative Approach*, (San Francisco: Chandler Publishing Co., 1962), p. 24.

2. Joseph Boskin and Robert A. Rosentone, "Introduction," *The Annals*, Vol. 382, (March 1969), p. ix.

3. "Protest in the Sixties," *The Annals*, Special Issue, (March 1969).

4. By-Laws, American College of Hospital Administration, adopted August 15, 1969.

5. *Code of Ethics*, American College of Hospital Administrators and American Hospital Association, adopted by Regents of the College and Trustees of Association, September 1957.

6. Jerome H. Skolnick, *The Politics of Protest, A Task Force Report* submitted to the National Commission on the Causes and Prevention of Violence, (New York: Simon and Schuster, 1969), p. 150.

7. Association of Black Social Workers, "Position Statement," presented at National Conference on Social Welfare, New York, May 26, 1969.

8. Charles L. Sanders, "The Growth of the Association of Black Social Workers," *Social Casework*, L1, (May 1970), p. 277.

9. Irwin Epstein, "Organizational Careers, Professionalization, and Social Worker Radicalism," *Social Service Review*, Vol. 44, June 1970, pp. 123-130.

10. Robert K. Merton, *Social Theory and Social Structure*, (New York: Free Press, 1957), pp. 195-206. Everett Hughes, "Institutional Office and the Person," *American Journal of Sociology*, Vol. XLIII, (1943), pp. 404-413.

11. Morris Rosenberg, et al., *Occupations and Values*, (Glencoe, Illinois: The Free Press, 1957) p. 27. Sigmund Nosow and William H. Form, *Man, Work and Society*, (New York: Basic Books, Inc., 1962).

12. Robert Presthus, *The Organizational Society*, (New York: Vintage Books, 1962), p. 247.

13. University Education for Administration in Hospitals; A Report of the Commission on University Education in Hospital Administration, 1954. (Washington, D.C.: American Council on Education). Russell E. Smith and Dorothy Zietz, *American Social Welfare Institutions*, (New York: John Wiley and Sons, Inc., 1970), p. 236.

14. Richard L. Durbin and W. Herbert Springall, *Organization and Administration of Health Care: Theory, Practice, Environment*, (St. Louis: C. V. Mosby Company, 1969).

15. Roger Klein, ed., *The Profession of Hospital Administration*, (Atlanta: Georgia Hospital Association, 1960).

16. Alvin W. Gouldner, "Cosmopolitans and Locals: Toward an Analysis of Latent Social Roles," *Administrative Science Quarterly*, Vols. II, III, December 1957, December 1958, pp. 201-306.

17. Lydia Rapport, "In Defense of Social Work: An Examination of Stress in the Profession," *Social Service Review*, March 1960, p. 63.

7 | NABSW's Tactical Areas for Dealing with Institutional Racism

WE SHALL NOW PRESENT ANSWERS TO the second question posed by this study: What tactical areas have been used by the newly-formed black professional organizations for dealing with racism? An assessment is made of the tactical operations of these emerging groups. As we use the term, "tactic" refers to the specific alternate action employed by the association for dealing with each specific form of racism. The tactical areas are actually areas of perception of institutional racism. Because of the various forms of racism which are perceived in the established white organizations, different groups may choose different approaches for dealing with the professional association's racist practices. Some may have protested, demonstrated, and confronted, while others may have taken independent directions for building more legitimate institutions.

This study does not assume that the major objective of the emerging black groups has been to change the established white organizations. Rather, the study aims to determine what the two emerging black groups, who as activists were challenging the status quo, have done about racism. While most of our research focused on the national groups, some illustrations are cited using local chapters.

TACTICAL AREAS. The subjects were interviewed regarding their efforts as to what the National Association of Black Social Workers was doing about the specific forms of racism, which were noted on the frequency scale for patterns of institutional racism. It would appear that the tactics most frequently developed among the social workers were conducted in the areas of Program Activity, Official Position, Goals, Membership, Role and Function, Conferences, and Organizational Values. The areas in which the least activity occurred were Staffing, Coalition and Alliance, Evaluation, Publications, Funding, Recruitment, Education and Training, and Scholarship and Awards.

There is a relationship between the tactical areas developed by social workers for dealing with racism and those forms of racism which they perceived in white associations. Those areas such as: Program Activity, Official Position, Goals, Membership, Role and Function, Conference, and Organizational Values in which frequent activity occurred were also the most frequently perceived forms of racism. At least 50 percent of the subjects had perceived each category.

Although other forms of racism had been significantly perceived, especially Staffing and Publications, none of these was among the major tactical areas employed by social workers.

Program Activity. Almost half of the subjects in this study noted that NABSW was developing a different type of program than in the white professional organization. They defined "professionalism" as having a responsibility for their oppressed "brothers and sisters," rather than being an elitist group of college graduates. According to them, the needs of the black community dictated that they include some direct services as a component of their organization rather than being only an organization to benefit members. In essence, this organization's program was a mixed type—servicing members and clients.

One leader cited that his national organization had no clear control over Program Activity as yet because NABSW is a new organization. He noted that the national organization advocated a strong local community orientation based on the particular needs, conditions, and decisions of specific communities and not a national one. The New York Chapter, as a local affiliate, has designed an Immigrant Program that provides for West Indians, Haitians, and Africans who are newcomers to the community. A strong sense of peoplehood and fraternity underlies the purpose of this service. Among other programs offered are:

Tutorial Program—provides after-school centers and educational services to pre-school and high school youth.

Child Development Center—provides day care services for families.

Assistance to black social work students in Inter-Council of Black Social Work Students.

Publications—bi-monthly Newsletter; Journal.

Technical Assistance—provides consultation and assistance to community groups.

Conferences—holds annual community conferences.

Afro-American Day Parade—provides planning and coordination of annual parade, emphasizing black heritage.

Although these programs exist, there are adversaries who consider these programs as "institution" based and the same kind of program services that the established white organizations would offer. Said one leader:

> Black organizations need to be involved in institutional control and control over institutions which serve them. Community control is more than just a black principal, but training parents to obtain community control and training them about a different curriculum.

Official Position on Social Issues. NABSW has developed activities that pertain to the Official Positions which an organization can take. These are instances wherein both national and local chapters clearly indicate their activism through a collective assertion on some issue which affects the total black community. For example, advertisements in the black press have been published setting forth positions on certain issues [1].

Examples of this tactic are illustrated through the position statements on: "Free Angela Davis" campaign, Nixon administration on welfare policies, and support of black candidates for mayor in Philadelphia and Newark. At the Third Annual Conference, resolutions were made denouncing the Bates bill, a legislative proposal which called for the sterilization of welfare mothers who continue to have children. Participants took a firm stance against "the establishment-sanctioned flow of narcotics into the black community through rampant heroin and barbiturate circulation which victimizes the innocent and allows the perpetrators of evil to continue to supply death to our people." [2]

At the same conference, the political stance of the

organization was clearly indicated when the National President resolved:

> President Nixon and his administration are anti-black, creating a repressive atmosphere which is near the brink of facism...Nixon is a representative of some of the people, rather than all of the people...Black people should run black politicians out of their communities if they continue to endorse Nixon. [3]

As a further indication of what the organization is doing regarding Positions on Social Issues, a subcommittee of the New York Chapter listed the priorities for the coming election year. It was stated that among them the NABSW would emphasize

> the utilization of the principles of collective leadership as a means of developing a strong, but diversified pool of leaders who would be able to take positions and speak on different issues. [4]

Role and Function. Among the social work leaders, fewer than half of them saw the organization's Role and Function as a new instrument for the black professional and client.

One leader observed:

> NABSW was created out of the need to establish the kind of social services that are relevant for black people. The priority of services has to be determined by the black community and the black professionals...Black social workers in the profession have a very different role to play, not only in developing services but in deciding what the profession is, what it should be, and in what direction it

should go...NABSW is changing the profession, because the profession is not based on action ... It's based upon a residual kind of approach where services or action comes after a breakdown. But it does nothing in terms of initiating action.

Another interviewee noted that

the National Association of Social Workers' function is to service the white professional. NABSW, as a black organization, is relating to a total black community and its people.

As a tactical area for action against racism, the Role and Function of NABSW was described by one leader as

a black organization involved in institutional control, as well as developing control over institutions which serve black people. White organizations have never addressed themselves to this issue; they have been building white institutions in the black community...NABSW as a black institution is collectively making its own plans, giving feedback from black to black as against white to white.

Another leader noted that

the organization's role was to deal with the consequences of racism, and not eradicating racism. We are protecting our own interests, so that racism does not continue to destroy the people...We are building a strong community...We have something that white institutions do not have and that is concern about working with all black groups; schools and economic development are our interests also. We want to build a strong community, strong nation, and establish ties with all African nations; we want to improve the collective black community since we suffer the same peculiar predicament.

Staffing Patterns. Staffing Patterns in NABSW, as an area for dealing with the racist practices, has not been handled. However, one of the leaders indicated that most of the white organization's boards, committees, consultants, and service staff reflect such a shortage of black people that this could be the only activity on which NABSW should work. But Staffing Patterns, even among the top governmental staff, reflects this racist pattern when only seventeen of the 100 United States Senators hire black secretaries or aides; only twenty-seven of the 435 Congressmen have black staff; and only two committees of the United States House of Representatives have a single black person on the staff. [5]

Initial actions by NABSW in dealing with the white professional hierarchy had showed that the National Conference on Social Welfare had increased its black representatives on the Executive Board from two to eight. This followed the confrontation during the tumultuous conference in 1969. [6]

Evaluation of Program. Black social work leaders had charged the established white professional organization with failure to use black input in effective techniques for evaluating their programs.

To overcome this racist indicator, about 40 percent of the NABSW leaders indicated that their broadly based membership in local chapters, such as those in Philadelphia and Detroit, allows for consumers or recipients of service to become members. Said one of the leaders:

The fact that we are accountable to our other oppressed brothers and sisters means we must listen to them.

The New York Chapter took cognizance of consumer participation in establishing two child development centers. The Board provides for the inclusion of mothers in operating and evaluating the services offered by the Centers. A Black Parent Advisory Group was also structured into the program. It was noted, however, that the consumers' participation did not preclude strains and differences in the group, nor the fact that the consumer may also perceive himself as a nonprofessional and is easily persuaded by the "majority opinion."

Perhaps the comment by one of the leaders more aptly described how one of the NABSW local affiliates related to the technique of evaluation through its use of consumer input:

We are relating more directly to the man on the street. Our open storefront operations allow for clients to be there all the time. They tell us straight out and they create an atmosphere where they immediately tell us what they think.

Coalitions and Alliances. At least 40 percent of the subjects recognized that NABSW had developed a tactic regarding the use of Coalitions and Alliances. While the predominantly white organizations had exerted little influence on other organizations in regard to minority groups, NABSW and many of its local affiliates were making use of this device.

The local affiliates, perhaps, provide more illustrations than the national organization in the use of coalitions. However, in the earlier stages of the organization's development, the NABSW, National Welfare Rights Organization, and Social Welfare Workers Movement collectively achieved the take-over of the general session of the NCSW's 1969 conference. This coalition stopped the officers and speakers from securing the platform until the coalition demands had been presented. Representatives from these groups were invited to join conference committees and extended invitations to nominate individuals for official committees. At the 1970 conference, four candidates were to be elected from these groups. By 1973, there were six black candidates for national office in the NCSW—out of twenty-two designated by the Nominating Committee.

On the local scene, the New York Chapter was a charter member and organizer of the United Federation of Black Community Organizations—as a black urban coalition. The chapter also allied with the black social work students in the New York area (comprising students from Adelphi, Columbia, Fordham, New York University, Hunter, and Rutgers Schools of Social Work) in order to make their impact on various aspects of social work education. These areas include: admissions, scholarships, faculty, and curriculum.

The NABSW Chicago Chapter has also expressed its willingness to "be involved in a front that, until now, no established white group would do." Its merger with the Southern Christian Leadership Conference's Operation Breadbasket and NWRO on certain issues, where they can come together as people with the same interests, indicated the usefulness of Coalitions and Alliances as a tactical device. SCLC and NABSW have supported local black elected officials and will endorse a black candidate for mayor of Chicago. In Syracuse, New York, the NABSW Chapter merged with the Black Employment Council, Black Dentists, and Black Lawyers' Fund to form the Coalition of Equality.

These actions are a reversal of the traditional, non-partisan stance held by social workers. Coalitions and Alliances do reflect a new found black unity wherein there is a degree of consensus among black social workers on issues, problems, and solutions with which the black community must deal.

Organizational Goals. The majority of those interviewed were able to support the national organization's goals as embodied in the NABSW Constitution and By-Laws:

> To promote the welfare and survival of the black community through black unity. Concerned black social workers state that black unity and survival must be predicated upon a national movement to organize and develop the black community. To achieve this goal, the black worker must recognize the crucial necessity of functioning in the black community as a servant of his people.

Chapters in Chicago, New York, Detroit, and Philadelphia are demonstrating their adherence to these goals and their allegiance to black survival and liberation through their activities in behalf of black people. All of these groups are to share responsibility for their community.

Organizational Values. The interviewees indicated that NABSW had instituted a different values base or philosophical stance in its organization. It was thus able to penetrate and reveal the entire racist aspect of the social welfare system and substitute other models which would free blacks.

The emphasis on promoting black nationalism as a philosophy was seen as a positive value which would give blacks some psychological sense of identity and participation. Fostering black self-interest and self-determination was seen as a continuation of the historical ethnic patterns and voluntary associations in American life. Embodied in the new values framework is the NABSW Code of Ethics. This code promotes basic tenets underlying the social worker's responsibility to his "brethren" and adherence to the extended-family concept. Loyalty to brotherhood comes before personal interest, according to the basic doctrine.

The black social workers, in essence, have substituted a values base which condemns established social welfare institutions as tools of oppression and adjustment. The organization is an instrument to help people liberate black people from playing so many roles in order to survive.

A new language permeates the new philosophical concepts: increased use of the words power, system, representative, liberation, survival, oppression, change agent, black and white, separation, and independence tend to show that a different set of issues is being faced by this organization.

In expressing the different philosophical base, one leader said:

> We are not involved with changing white organizations—we have stopped looking at what they are doing or not doing. . .We are about what we are doing. . .We are not reacting but defining and taking care of business. The organizations are about activism on a local level.

Funding Sources. As a national organization, the NABSW's current funding comes primarily from the financial assessment of its 22 chapter affiliates and the annual conferences. Each chapter is assessed $2.00 per member per year for national dues. Each chapter pays $100.00 per year to affiliate with the National Office, with the exception of student chapters, which pay a membership fee of $25.00 per year. Allowances have also been made for individuals who are not in a locality where there is a chapter. They pay only $5.00 per year directly to the national office.

The local chapter also provides some indication of what is being done to deal with the racist aspects of the budget in white organizations. It had been recognized that black social welfare institutions were almost nonexistent and consequently they received no public funds compared to those utilized by the white community.

Local chapters in New York City and Syracuse, in addition to their own membership fees and other fund raising sources, have been able to secure local government money for programs. Two Day Care Centers were established in the New York area under a grant sponsored by the Department of Social Services. In few instances, appeals have been made to white foundations for financial support by the local chapters. There is a doctrine that black-owned and -developed institutions must be supported predominantly by black people. Fund raising committees are actively conducting programs in economic development, holding dances, and developing program proposals for public funds as sources of money for NABSW chapters.

Membership. In dealing with the racism perceived in the Membership Patterns of the predominantly white professional organizations, NABSW membership has been reformed in several ways.

More than half of those questioned (60 percent) indicated that this was a pattern in which concerned attention was given. The membership is more broadly based; that is, it aims to include rather than to exclude people. Said some of the leaders:

We have paraprofessionals on the same level with professionals. They can operate and fulfill any role in which they feel capable of producing.

NASW stresses professionalism which is an elite type of thinking. NABSW has not set up an elitist type of organization. All blacks working in the social service field are included, which means clerks, secretaries, and maintenance staff. We are advocating black communalism, which is a family type of thing.

Regardless of credentials, we have those interested in social welfare concerns. Social workers and others are provided a vehicle to become involved in a meaningful way; to plan action and take action which they did not have in NASW.

Since all black social workers are affected equally by racism, although whites tend to say the opposite by claiming that all "professional" social workers have the option of membership. We feel that there are different levels of commitment to the black struggle. We must utilize our membership in the way that they feel that they can best use others to fulfill the goals of the organization.

According to the Constitution and By-laws, the criteria for membership represent one of the primary differences between the white social welfare organizations and NABSW in terms of the racist patterns in Membership.

Publications. Another area in which NABSW had not developed a tactic for dealing with racism is in Publications. Because Publications was one of the most frequently perceived racist patterns in the white organizations, one would expect it to be an area in which the organization would promptly initiate its own published materials. While the national organization is still in the process of securing funding for its publishing vehicle, the New York Chapter has sponsored a semiannual journal. The journal, *Black Caucus*, was established as a forum for dealing with social issues in the black community. [7] The journal is broadly based on issues in health, education, and welfare, and is in the process of being officially sponsored as the national publication. According to one respondent:

> Where *Social Work* accepts articles which advance the white position, *Black Caucus* accepts articles which pertain to the black community.

Conferences. About one-third of those we polled indicated that NABSW Conference activities seemed more responsive to the interests and needs of its black constituency. The conferences have related to such issues as jobs, housing, and employment which affect black people. According to the subjects, there are several aspects of Conferences which reflect some innovation. The planning, participants, program content, and structure of the conferences represent a different tactic than those of the white, established professional associations. Various local Chapters of the NABSW have been responsible for planning and operating the three national conferences held in Philadelphia, Washington, and Chicago. [8]

The conferences have been geared toward implementing ideas through the State Caucus which deal with specific local and state wide conferences.

Recruitment. The NABSW Recruitment Patterns have been closely related to its membership campaign. Membership is sought from a broadly-based segment of black social service workers, students, and other persons who accept the Constitution and By-laws of the NABSW. [9] Membership in NABSW should indicate a willingness to

> work for and support the objectives of the association; attend membership meetings and national, general conferences; serve on committees; and, pay annual dues as prescribed in the Constitution and By-laws. [10]

Personnel in public welfare settings have been a major source of recruitment in view of the large group of minority persons employed in public welfare. As a national, incorporated organization with tax-exempt status, the NABSW now has twenty-two Chapters as financial official affiliates.

The student population has been a vital source for recruitment. An Office of Student Affairs was established by the Constitution since black social work students are another population whose goals and values appear to coincide with the NABSW. In fact, NABSW was a student-inspired organization from its beginning in 1967.

Education and Training. Consistent with the low perception of racism in Education and Training, black social workers' activities have been minor in developing tactics for dealing with the area. With the exception of the educational component in Conferences and Publications, there appears to be no permanent organizational structure on the national level for dealing with the Educational aspect of social work from a black perspective. Educational issues have been consistently confronted by various subcommittees on an ad hoc basis on the national level.

The local chapters provide a more visible means for dealing with educational matters related to black social workers. For example, the Black Student Social Work Council and NABSW, New York Chapter, have correlated their efforts in meeting with deans and admissions personnel to get more blacks admitted to Schools of Social Work in the New York area. They have protested racist policies and practices regarding admissions and scholarship procedures. They have innovated new minority content in curricula in order to remove myths and distortions about blacks.

Currently, the NABSW is considering the development of a National Institute of Black Social Thought. This institute conceivably would be the hub for all educational and training programs and issues related to blacks in social work. [11]

The NABSW strategy for a more relevant Education and Training program has been minimal in its emerging development. Although NABSW is concerned with educational issues, this is not the association's chief area of concern. It does deal with these issues when they pertain to blacks' educational opportunities. Perhaps some of the issues this organization raised regarding social work education have been more vigorously pursued by the Council on Social Work Education, whose main function is to deal with social work education issues. In the Council's recent reports concerning minority representation in the graduate student body for the 1971-72 year, 14.9 percent were black, having increased from 888 in the 1969-70 year to 1,067. In the 1971-72 year, 12.2 percent of the full-time faculty were black, rising to 276 from 259 in 1970-71. Ethnic characteristics of the increasing number of graduating students are not available; but of the doctoral students in 1970-71, one of four was non-white, including fifty-four blacks. The proportion of black doctoral students had risen from 8.9 percent in 1969-70 to 11.7 percent in 1970-71. [12]

It is evident then that the issues relative to blacks in social work education are being considered. NABSW, as an emerging organization, has had a strategic role initially in doing something about Education. It was one of the groups who did raise the hard-and-fast questions and issues. This spearheaded the thrust for developing a national perspective for minority affairs in social work education by the CSWE.

Scholarship and Awards. The NASW developed no specific formal Scholarships or Awards program for its membership or any other recipients aside from the intrinsic and psychological rewards one receives.

Incentives can often be the means for sustaining motivation in an organization. According to March and Simon, an individual's contribution to an organization is based upon the service or inducements made by the organization. [13] Following this principle, the issue of the membership's participation on a sustained basis is questionable, when there may not be any tangible benefits such as Scholarship and Awards to be received.

NOTES

1. Statement on Black Rebellion, *Amsterdam News,* October 21, 1967. Position Statement: Community Control and Decentralization, November 25, 1968, (Files of NABSW, New York City Chapter).

2. National Association of Black Social Workers, Annual Conference, Chicago, Illinois, *Amsterdam News,* April 6, 1971, p. 8.

3. C. J. Williams, National President: speech delivered at National Conference of Black Social Workers, Chicago, Ill., April 4, 1971.

4. Letter: Ad Hoc Committee for Alternate Leadership, April 20, 1971.

5. Simeon Booker, "Ticker Tape U.S.A.," *Jet*, XL, (March 25, 1971), p. 11.

6. John C. Kidneigh, "The New York Conference Story," *Social Welfare Forum*, (New York: Columbia University Press, 1969), pp. 178-184.

7. See: *Black Caucus journal*, Association of Black Social Workers, Volumes I, II, III, (New York City Chapter, Publications Committee).

8. "The Black Family," National Conference of Black Social Workers, Philadelphia, Pa., February 21-23, 1969. "The Black Social Worker: A New Dimension," National Conference of Black Social Workers, Washington, D.C., February 22-25, 1970. "Blueprints for Black Unity," National Conference of Black Social Workers, Chicago, Ill., April 1-4, 1971.

9. Constitution and By-Laws of the National Association of Social Workers, revised 1970.

10. *Ibid.*, p. 2

11. Howard Stanback, "Proposal: National Institute of Black Social Thought," National Association of Black Social Workers, July 1971. (Mimeographed).

12. *Statistics on Social Work Education, 1970*, (New York: Council on Social Work Education, 1971). *Statistics on Social Work Education, 1971*, (New York: Council on Social Work Education, 1971).

13. James G. March and Herbert A. Simon, *Organizations*, (New York: John Wiley & Sons, Inc.), 1961.

8 | NAHSE's Tactical Areas for Dealing with Institutional Racism

BOTH THE WHITE PROFESSIONAL health associations and the health care delivery system provide ample sources for assessing NAHSE's tactical areas for dealing with the racism in health institutions. The following indictment of racism in these institutions surely indicates the urgency of devising effective counter tactics:

1. The goal of all people working in health institutions can never be simply the expansion and perpetuation of these institutions. The goal must be the best possible health for all people by whatever means necessary.

2. The basic health statistics show that this aim has not been accomplished in this country. Health in 1968 in the United States of America is a racially distributed commodity.

3. The failure of the institutions to correct this injustice can be traced partly to the fact that the system rations health according to purchasing power rather than need. But more basically, these institutions fail because their control is vested in an essentially closed panel of *white*

professionals who are not representative of all health professionals, let alone all patients who are to be served. This lack of representation allows bigotry in a few cases and ignorance in most cases to prevail at decision making levels and results in actions which have racist results. *Until black people have some control of the decisions which directly affect their health and health care, the white health institutions will continue to support the overall pattern of institutional racism.* [Italics added.] [1]

The tactics which were most frequently employed by the health administrators in developing a new organization involved Recruitment, Education and Training, Staffing, Role and Function, Membership, Coalition and Alliance, Funding, Organizational Values, and Organizational Goals. The areas which received less attention during these initial years were Official Position on Social Issues, Evaluation, Scholarship and Awards, and Publications.

Recruitment. Among the health administrators, the majority responded to Recruitment as an area in which NAHSE has developed an alternate plan for rectifying the problem of racism in the health management field. The interrelationship between Recruitment, Membership, and Education and Training is very apparent in these major efforts by NAHSE. Recruitment is a number one strategical area for NAHSE for several reasons: first, blacks have not participated in significant numbers as providers; second, black health providers have struggled under handicaps to extend meager resources to the greatest number of consumers, but yet they are underrepresented in major health policy decisions; third, health is the second largest industry in the country and minority manpower needs more representation; and fourth, in order to effect change for oppressed people, a major way is to increase the supply of minority health management personnel.

NAHSE has taken steps to attract more suitable candidates to the field of health administration and to its own professional association. The established white professional association heretofore has exerted little activity in finding, selecting, and providing financial support to potential minority candidates to health administration.

College Recruitment. In order to implement its recruitment tactics, NAHSE has collaborated with the Association of University Programs in Hospital Administration (AUPHA) and the American Hospital Association (AHA). NAHSE solicited these organizations and gained supportive funds for establishing A Summer Experience in Health Careers during 1970 for the first time. [2] The report outlined a more exhaustive and evaluative approach for the succeeding year. During the next year, NAHSE visited campuses of predominantly black colleges in order to recruit forty students. The project was conducted in New York City and Baltimore. Ten students from this summer program were enrolled in another internship in mental health hospitals under the New York State Department of Mental Hygiene during the summer, 1971.

During the second year, the Summer Recruitment Program expanded from two to five cities and from forty to seventy-one students. [3]

Following are the cities and number of students participating:

Baltimore . . . . 8 students
Chicago . . . . .17 students
Newark . . . . 7 students
New York . . . . .27 students

Philadelphia . . . . 3 students
N. Y. State
Department of
Mental Hygiene . . . .10 students

The program was designed for twelve weeks especially to attract juniors and seniors with interest in hospital and health administration. Minority students were given a stipend from $135 to $150 a week. At least $85 to $100 of this amount was contributed by the hospital. [4]

Through these recruitment activities, NAHSE has involved the established white professional associations to achieve its purposes, and has stimulated program activity for these organizations as well. Although there was initial resistance, NAHSE held meetings and arranged oral and visual presentations in order to have these groups endorse and collaborate on these programs.

Employment Opportunities. NAHSE has maintained a function of providing information on employment opportunities available in health management. It has become a clearinghouse for positions open to blacks primarily. NAHSE is assisting in filling the vacuum in minority manpower because of its black consciousness in hiring blacks.

A recruitment plan was developed as a visual aid instrument for personnel in hospital and health care administration. A film entitled "Soul" has been used in conferences in schools and colleges in order to orient persons to health management. The "Fixing Business" was developed by AUPHA featuring the President of NAHSE. It was an innovation in the use of training aids. Another filmstrip on "Health Careers from a Black Perspective" has been developed for distribution and sale.

Because many black students have no conception of health administration, NAHSE visits high schools to acquaint the guidance counselors and students with the opportunities in the health field.

Student Affiliates. In February, 1971, a student affiliate of NAHSE was organized at the annual conference in Chicago. The student affiliate is an organization composed of black and other minority group students in various programs of hospital and health care administration in the country. National officers were selected and various regions established—Eastern, Midwestern, and Western. The purpose, goals, and tactics for the organization were outlined in their position paper. [5]

In order to effect their goals, the students outlined the following means:

> Coordinate our efforts with other existing organizations committed to similar goals. Develop a model delivery system that can achieve these goals. Insure that all our efforts, be they successful or failures, be shared with others striving toward the same end. Bring all existing resources to bear on the effective resolution of these problems. Recruit black and other people of color into the whole gamut of health care professions, especially health care administration. Bring to the awareness of all people the existing expertise, skills, technology, and methodology in order to translate the theory of equality in health care into reality.

These Recruitment activities indeed reflect a reversal of pattern of some ten years ago when minority persons interested in health administration, already showing leadership potential, had to take jobs outside of the country, take jobs as senior housekeepers in a hospital, or a younger person may have been directed by his guidance counselor to go into the ministry. These current programs now encourage, stimulate, and finance minority students to enter the health field.

Education and Training. Not only has NAHSE developed efforts to innovate and reform patterns of Recruitment, but its efforts in the area of Education and Training reflect this. As a tactic for dealing with the racist aspects of the health system, NAHSE is providing solutions to major racial and health manpower problems. Through NAHSE efforts, a health administration curriculum has been initiated at a major black university for the first time. The development of a program is in progress at Howard University because of its related Schools of Medicine, Business, Law, and Social Work.

Because of NAHSE's aggressive recruitment program for training blacks in health administration, its exchanges and collaboration with AUPHA were intensified. Admissions policies and financial aid programs at all schools have been re-examined with the aim of attracting more minority students into the field. NAHSE has conducted a survey of the number of minority students in programs of health administration. According to the report, among the forty schools of hospital administration in the U.S.A., there are at least 1700 students enrolled. Forty-five of these students are black. During the 1969-1970 academic year, only three blacks were graduated from schools of hospital administration. [6] Consequently, NAHSE has provided input regarding the number of minority students, and the means for increased admissions. It has also located students for these programs, and worked on special programs in conjunction with the AUPHA and individual universities.

Scholarship Assistance. NAHSE has developed a Whitney M. Young, Jr. Educational Trust Fund for students pursuing graduate education in health administration. The purpose of the Fund is to defray educational expenses for blacks in graduate programs. The Trust Fund is financed by contributions based on a sliding scale of salaries among NAHSE members; outside sources are also solicited.

Health Education. NAHSE has sensitized the public, government, and industry to the needs of the disadvantaged and poor in health care. The organization was responsible for the "Position Paper on Health and the Black Condition," representing the official stand to be taken by the Black Caucus of the Congress on Health.

Professional and Continuing Education. NAHSE proposed as one of its own tactics that it would "promote continuing educational experiences to its members through seminars, workshops, and other means." [7]

Exchange Programs. Plans are being initiated between the John F. Kennedy Medical Center, Liberia, Africa and NAHSE to develop an exchange program in nursing, x-ray and medical technology, and other allied health fields.

Membership. In examining what NAHSE has done about its Membership pattern as a means of combating racism, its Constitution and By-Laws set forth the criteria for membership. [8] There is a basic relationship between the tactics in Membership, Recruitment, and Education and Training. For example, in the effort to recruit more persons and especially students, the student organization was established within NAHSE, as was discussed under Recruitment. The criteria for membership, dues structure, and procedure for processing new members are outlined. The composition of the organization's membership has not been resolved. At one point, it was proposed that a variety of specialists in the decision-making positions in health, such as hospital administration, nursing, nutrition, and non-credential administration would belong to NAHSE. In another instance, classes of membership were proposed such as, full participating, associate, affiliate, and student. The former three types were not ratified.

As a newly-emerging organization, NAHSE has conducted a manpower survey on black health administrators including minority students enrolled in the forty different schools. [9]

Coalition and Alliance. Following the tactics for Recruitment, Education and Training, and Membership, the area of Coalition and Alliance has seen a preponderance of activity. From the founding of NAHSE, it was apparent that this would be one of its immediate tactical areas. The Charter illustrates this significantly:

> To accomplish its goals, NAHSE will develop a genuine *partnership* between the existing health care system—those who recognize the need for change and those who have valuable input necessary for that change. [Italics added.]

This statement, in essence, underlies the organization's thrust to ally with any meaningful resource which can help to achieve NAHSE's prescribed ends. NAHSE has collaborated with groups and agencies in both the black and white communities. The groups have included the National Medical Association, Black Caucus of the American Public Health Association, Telethon for Research in Sickle Cell Anemia, Inc., American Hospital Association, American College of Hospital Administrators, and Association of University Programs in Hospital Administration.

The significance of working with the established, white

professional associations was so strongly felt, that NAHSE's Constitution and By-Laws provided for a Joint Committee of AHA and NAHSE. [10] The duties, membership, meetings, and officers of this Committee were outlined. This, in essence, provided a strategy for continuous confrontation on issues. It would help improve communication, quality of health to disadvantaged population, and inner city health institutions.

In addition to this Joint Committee, NAHSE members are serving on the Board of Trustees, Committees, and Councils of AHA. At the AHA conferences, NAHSE members have achieved greater involvement as Presiding Officers. Through these committees, NAHSE members are also AHA members, providing black input in formulating health policies.

While the NAHSE members in this study may not have openly perceived the role of Coalition and Alliance in racism, either to perpetuate or combat it, NAHSE's ideological framework has included this tactic. NAHSE's efforts to develop coalitions and cooperative activities with other organizations have resulted in positive relationships. Many of these establishment organizations have been able to extend their programs and gain access to the black community by developing these collateral actions with NAHSE.

Organizational Goals. As another professional, voluntary association, NAHSE's Goals indicate aims quite different from those in the established, white professional organizations.

NAHSE is concerned with the problems of both the black health consumer and provider. It is a change-oriented organization, which aims to alter the inequities in the health system which minorities encounter. Consequently, NAHSE's Goals were created within the context of combating racism. At the outset, it developed resolutions for dealing with the health services and manpower deficiencies which have accrued to blacks and other minorities. The following Goals have been stated for the organization:

1. To assist in devising methods to improve the delivery of health care to deprived black people as well as other minority races.

2. To insure that deprived black people and the poor receive care with the same dignity afforded more fortunate citizens.

3. To bring about the participation as providers and decision-makers of significant numbers of black men and women in the health field. [11]

Even though the leaders in this study may not have openly perceived the white organizations as racist, NAHSE Goals reflect the degree of black consciousness which this organization has been designed to carry out.

In order to implement Goals 1 and 2, NAHSE works with the AHA Joint Committee to Evaluate Hospital Standards. The implementation of Goal 3, relating to activity in the recruitment field, has been NAHSE's main thrust. This might be expected in view of the fact that it is a new organization needing to increase its membership, as well as blacks in the profession.

Conferences. During its initial years of operation, NAHSE has held its separate national conferences during the annual meetings of the American Hospital Association and the American College of Hospital Administrators held in Houston and Chicago in 1970 and 1971. [12] At these meetings, NAHSE's main objective has been toward furthering its own national development as an organization through expansion of membership and program development. Other meetings have also been held in Baltimore, Maryland. [13]

While members of NAHSE participated in the sessions of the established white organization, its own conference program included speakers, official business reports from officers of NAHSE, and programs in conjunction with AHA and ACHA.

Program Activity. There is an obvious interrelationship between Program Activity, Recruitment, Education and Training, Membership, and Coalition and Alliance as tactical areas. The latter can be viewed as sub-elements of Program Activity since they have been the major organizational activities. Both Recruitment and Education and Training have been the chief programs provided for in NAHSE's budgeted operating expenses.

Through NAHSE's own program and planning it has stimulated joint program activity between some of the established white organizations such as AHA and AUPHA. Aspects of these programs were discussed in Education and Training and Coalition and Alliance.

Staffing. NAHSE has set as one of its major objectives:

> . . .to insure that meaningful input from black health care administrators, providers, and consumers be incorporated in the decision-making process relating to the development of all new programs and the profession of health services to the black community. [14]

In order to implement this, it has had confrontation with AHA and AUPHA regarding their Staffing patterns.

NAHSE also helps through its executive job placement service to provide minority staff persons to various job openings.

NAHSE has moved beyond focusing simply on the inequities in staffing of professional associations and health management positions in service institutions. Many of the locals of NAHSE have actively recruited for minority participation on the boards of trustees of voluntary organizations. [15]

Funding. The fact that NAHSE makes use of various financial resources in order to conduct its program is consistent with their lack of perception of racism among Funding Sources. The organization states that to accomplish its goals it will "seek necessary financial resources to support these goals." This means that the sources may be membership, government, foundations, and the corporate structure.

To illustrate various sources of funding which NAHSE has rallied, the "Summer Recruitment Program," which was discussed in Education and Training, is a useful indicator. Funding sources for this program have ranged from private to federal sources. These included: the National Urban Coalition, Kellogg Foundation, Milbank Foundation, Wiebold Foundation, Commonwealth Fund, Weire Foundation, and Central Booklyn Model Cities.

NAHSE, in an effort to establish its own separate organization, proposed a $100,000 operating budget for an office. Membership funds and grants from private and public sources were envisioned as the primary means of support. Foundations such as Sloan, Milbank, Kellogg, and the established AHA were also contacted.

A paid, full-time executive directorship, responsible for funding sources, proposals and program development was established in conjunction with the AHA. The AHA, New York Office, in turn, has provided the funds and office space for the position on a half-time basis in order to assist NAHSE in becoming an ongoing organization. The same person also works half-time for AHA.

Official Position on Social Issues. As a national organization, NAHSE's tactic for developing Official Position on Social Issues has been almost negligible. This is understandable in view of the extensive use of negotiation and confrontation made through its coalitions and cooperative ventures with other groups and agencies. Additionally, until June 1971, the organization had been functioning without paid staff to operate a national office.

Nevertheless, NAHSE's use of Official Position as a tactic was exemplified by its work with the National Urban League regarding National Health Insurance, as well as the total American health care system. [16] In examining the poor and minority health care needs, it was NAHSE's endorsement that "the quality, quantity, and distribution of health services delivery, financing, and education required an urgent comprehensive approach." Other positions have included a position statement made to the Congressional Black Caucus regarding health conditions as they relate to blacks. [17]

On a local level, Chapters of NAHSE have taken strong stands on specific issues. As an example, the New York Chapter took issue with the New York City Health and Hospitals Corporation's omission of blacks and other minorities in influential decision-making positions within the Corporation. This was considered crucial, in view of the fact that more than 45 percent of the health consumers which the Corporation services are black. [18] An internal Equal Opportunities Council was recommended, as well as individual candidates for senior positions in the Corporation. NAHSE also solicited additional agencies, groups, and concerned citizens to support its position.

Evaluation; Publications; Scholarships and Awards. These three areas are the primary ones in which NAHSE has not developed *major* tactics during its three years of operation. There is evidence, however, that there is some activity in these areas. For example, NAHSE participation on the AHA Joint Committee (discussed earlier in its use of Coalition and Alliance) provides an instrumentality for assessing direct health services, so that racist elements are minimized. Among the duties of the Committee, the following pertain to Evaluation in that assessments and recommendations are to be made:

> . . .to make recommendations aimed at *elevating* the *quality* of health care services rendered to poor people and members of minority groups.

> . . .to make recommendations designed to *improve* the quality of health care services rendered in institutions serving predominantly disadvantaged populations. [19]

Publication. Although the organization has not developed any of its own separate publications, one article on the Association has appeared in a professional medical journal. [20]

Scholarships and Awards. While NAHSE has not fully developed or operated its own Scholarship Program, the initial procedures for this have begun. The Whitney M. Young, Jr. Educational Trust Fund was discussed under Education and Training as one of NAHSE's tactics. One of the main accomplishments in relation to Scholarships has been its major recruitment activities resulting in a number of minority students being placed in schools. NAHSE's Educational Committee provides assistance in locating scholarships for these students. NAHSE secured the support of AUPHA and the Kellogg Foundation for summer programs and scholarships for universities. Kellogg provided $306,130 in a grant to AUPHA for a national program to expand educational opportunities.

No formal annual Awards program has been instituted by NAHSE. Various individuals, however, have been cited for their contributions and other assistance. An example of this was the testimonial and award occasion sponsored by the NAHSE Student Organization in August 1971 for the Chairman of the Education Committee, Haynes Rice, who directed many of NAHSE's major programs in Recruitment and Education and Training.

Organizational Values. NAHSE has made use of certain Organizational Values as a tactic in developing a separate organization. We can assess certain important tenets to determine which Organizational Values best characterize the organization. First, NAHSE expresses its values forcefully through its statement on commitment in its Consitution. Inherent in the values is a concern first for the consumer who is served by institutions managed by minority members. There we see a sense of brotherhood, self-interest, peoplehood—which are Values held by every ethnic group, but newly emphasized by blacks. Second, there is a commitment to improving relationships among all persons in health management (social fraternalization). Third, there is the commitment for improving the education for minority health management personnel (education and progress). Fourth, the organization encourages minority races to enter the profession (self-interest, self-determination, and progress). Fifth, NAHSE is committed to providing continuing education to its members (education, motivation, mobility, and progress). Finally, NAHSE is concerned with combating discrimination against minorities in both the provision and administration of health care services (equality and democratic theory).

The organization is conditioned by these cultural values and dominant themes, which identify its role within society. Given all of these commitments it is apparent that NAHSE has developed a values system which embodies many of the current "American" values such as progress, equality, education, and motivation—apparently to be inculcated by black Americans as they impinge upon the health system.

Role and Function. Actually, this dimension set the basic tone as to what would be NAHSE's chief concerns. Contrary to some of the established, white, voluntary professional associations, NAHSE's tactic for dealing with racism within the health system was to establish a separate, ethnic-based organization. Its primary purpose is to elevate the quality of health care services rendered to the disadvantaged and the poor. The organization serves the dual function of relating to the needs of black consumers and providers, as stated in a Preamble to a position paper:

> The providers represent a broad cross-section of those who have been offering health care to the black population and, further, the consumer represents those who have felt the shortages of health services imposed upon them by our present system. [21]

NAHSE's Role and Function was conceived primarily to deal with a black agenda. Its progress and Organizational Values reflect the need for which it started. While the organization's function is not to offer health services directly, it has moved to participate at decision-making levels so that it can influence the actions in the health field which have significance for black providers and consumers. Its Role and Function may have initially related to the gaps in the white professional associations, but as the organization developed there were reform implications for the practice and study of health administration. Not only is a new role being suggested for the health administrators, but the health training curriculum has been criticized because of its irrelevance to the practice of health management in the inner city community.

NOTES

1. Knowles and Prewitt, *op. cit.*, p. 114.

2. Robert R. Detore, "Recommendations for the National Work Study Recruitment Program in Hospital Administration for Minority Group Members," Association of Univeristy Programs in Hospital Administration, Washington, D.C., 1971. (Mimeographed)

3. Haynes Rice, "Proposed Summer Recruitment Plan," submitted by Educational Committee, NAHSE, Baltimore, May 1971. (Mimeographed)

4. *Ibid.*

5. Position Paper: The Student Affiliates of the NAHSE, Chicago, Illinois, February 27, 1971.

6. "Program for Strengthened Graduate Programs of Business for Blacks with Interest in the Non-Profit Sector," (Exhibit B), NAHSE Education Committee, Baltimore, Md., February 1971. (Mimeographed)

7. *Amsterdam News*, Vol. 61, No. 34, August 21, 1971, p. 37.

8. Constitution and By-Laws, Article II, *ibid.*

9. Henry J. White, *Roster of the NAHSE and Member Status in American College of Hospital Administrators*, July 1970. (Mimeographed) Haynes Rice, *Proposed Budget for NAHSE*, February 1971. (Mimeographed)

10. Constitution and By-Laws, NAHSE, National Headquarters, Baltimore, Md., revised, September 1970.

11. Position Paper, NAHSE, *ibid.*

12. Meeting Agenda, NAHSE, Houston, Texas, September 1970. Meeting Agenda, NAHSE, Chicago, Illinois, February 26, 1971.

13. Minutes of Meeting, NAHSE, Provident Hospital, Baltimore, Maryland, June 12, 1971.

14. NAHSE, *Brochure for Membership,* National Headquarters, Baltimore, Md., June 1971.

15. Interview with Joseph Mann, President, NAHSE, New York Chapter, Brooklyn, N. Y., July 7, 1970.

16. "Toward A National Health Program," National Urban League Position, February 1971.

17. Position Paper: "Health and Black Conditions," NAHSE, Baltimore, Md. Submitted to Congressional Black Caucus, March 1971 (unpublished).

18. Position Paper: NAHSE, N. Y. Chapter, submitted to New York City Health and Hospitals Corporation, August 1971.

19. *Ibid.,* NAHSE, Constitution and By-Laws.

20. Sanders, "Black Assertion Among Black Professionals," *op. cit.*

21. Position Paper, NAHSE, September 1968 (unpublished).

9 | Comparing the Tactics of NABSW and NAHSE

IN COMPARING THE ORGANIZED ACTIONS of the social workers and health administrators, those tactics which had involved the most frequently similar activity among both groups are used as a starting point. We found these tactical areas in which there were similar actions: Goals, Membership, Role and Function, Conferences, and Organizational Values.

Goals. The finding among perceptions of institutional racism indicated that the social workers had perceived racism in the white organization's goals. Consistent with this, they developed efforts to deal with racism among white organizations by establishing their own Organizational Goals. NABSW set as its primary goal, the promotion of the welfare and survival of the black community through black unity. Implicit in this goal is the recognition that communal service will be offered. There is, therefore, a strong community service orientation, particularly in terms of working with other indigenous black organizations. It would seem that the social workers are dealing with the psychological phenomenon of black identity and through a strong sense of self, a more coherent, stronger, common, ethnic identity is developed which will have its psychological and political implications for blacks as a sub-dominant group of people.

NAHSE has established goals which are stated in terms of eliminating the inequities in services for black consumers and the inequities in position and opportunities for black health providers. Yet its members evinced no significant perception of racism in the white associations' goals. They did, however, question the Role and Function of the white organizations.

Both NABSW and NAHSE reflect a common effort to deal with Goals by having their organization direct some of its benefits to blacks. Inherent in both groups' stated Goals is a strong sense of community orientation and concern for black consumers of service.

Membership. As a means of dealing with the racist manifestations shown in white, social welfare organizations, the social workers have established more equitable criteria for Membership. There is a re-examination of the concept "professional." Persons employed in the field of social services, graduates of schools of social work, or students enrolled in a graduate school of social work can become members. This is considered a more inclusive rather than exclusive criterion for membership. As a younger, more outspoken, nationalistic group, NABSW seemed more committed to the principles of democratic representation and equitable participation.

NAHSE had not finalized its membership criteria. Its membership includes persons who are experienced and trained in health management or students in this field. Health executives are distinguished from nursing administrators, management personnel in housekeeping, or dieticians in a health institution.

As an organization, NAHSE's main thrust in the tactical area of Membership has been to define who can belong, based solely on education and practice in health administration, and to establish a dues structure of $40 per year. Because of the small number of minority persons in health administration, greater efforts have been centered on attracting and recruiting persons to schools of hospital and health care management. Although blacks have experienced alienation in the field, NAHSE's membership policy provided for inclusion of non-black persons who are "qualified." "Qualified" as a criterion in this instance parallels the white organization in the sense of education ("qualified") being the base for membership. Essentially, this a "professional" organization, which has not yet devised ways for various levels or division of labor for nonprofessional personnel to participate on a permanent basis, except for pre-professional or professional students in training in the field. They did, however, rate Membership highly as a manifestation of racism, and it would have been expected that clearer membership policies would have developed.

Role and Function. This was highly perceived by the social workers as an indicator of institutional racism. They questioned the basis for the white association and, in some instances, their failure to become members was based on the organization's irrelevancy to the black community. It would be expected then that the social workers would tend to develop an organization whose Role and Function would more clearly reflect the needs of black clients and professionals in the black community. The following premises underlie NABSW activity: 1) clients can be served more effectively by their services which are based on the client's articulated needs; 2) these services can be offered by blacks who are more familiar with black life styles; 3) there is a need for more black participation in deciding, planning, and serving the black community. With these premises, NABSW's tactic has been one of providing services and organizing strong coalitions on a local level among black groups.

In contrast to the health administrators the social workers speak of organizing a strong black community, which reflects their activist orientation. The nature of health administration and NAHSE's initial organizing process have inhibited dealing with the community as such, although health administration does indeed have a political aspect as does all administrative behavior. But the health administrators seemingly chose to deal politically almost exclusively within the current health system by working with AHA, ACHA, and AUPHA, as well as black groups.

NAHSE, in creating tactics around Role and Function, has developed an organization to deal with health care delivery as it affects blacks, and with securing jobs for blacks in the health system. While primary tactics have been directed toward the professional organizations, NAHSE has questioned the merits of health administration as a discipline. There are gaps in services and in the profession that could not be bridged by the white associations, such as Recruitment, especially with the professional images necessary for increasing and liberating the self-identity inherent in black oppression.

NAHSE considers as part of its Role and Function the questioning of professional training for a health management career, leading to consideration of a curriculum, more relavent to the black experience in health administration, to be introduced in major black universities. There are unique features in dominantly black health institutions and patients, which need to be incorporated in the training and curriculum wherever blacks are being prepared to work with black patients.

The social workers' questioning of education resulted in their unique proposal for an Institute of Social Thought.

The health administrators' interest in establishing health management curricula at black universities is also indicative of a "new health management." Erber observed in describing the role of professional associations that

> a professional association rarely plays an important part in determining the professional roles of its members. These roles are determined by the clients of the professional or in the case of the bureaucratic professional by his employer. In other words, the future role of planners is going to be determined largely by the cities and other political bodies which hire them as employees or consultants. [1]

The Role and Function dimension of these new black organizations dictates their consciousness with black clients and the uniqueness of the black bureaucratic health institution in which these providers are employed. In contrast to Erber's statement, it would seem that these black professional organizations do play a part in determining the role dimensions of the social worker and health administrator.

In general, then, both groups have developed their organization's Role and Function so that it would more specifically reflect their own needs and interests as black professionals with some sense of community responsibility.

Publications. Following their high perception of racism in the area of the Publications of the white, established associations, the black social workers proposed a semiannual journal and regular newsletters. An official printed medium, other than a periodic newsletter, has not yet developed from a national perspective. The problem of securing a paid staff for production and circulation of such materials is the major constraint. While the local New York Chapter produced a semiannual journal for an initial two years, the lack of paid staff for professional direction in production and circulation saw these efforts slowly abate during the third year. "Seed" money was never secured from private foundations although appeals were made.

The health administrators did not perceive racism Publications as strongly as social workers and therefore conducted no major activity in this area.

Although their activity is minimal, the social workers are perhaps better able to give a greater emphasis because they depend more on written materials. The profession also involves an older and more conceptualized discipline in terms of training, curriculum, and professional associations. Both social workers and health administrators are engaged in primarily "doing- and activity-oriented" disciplines; this could contribute, especially with an activist group, to giving less emphasis to Publications. In new organizations it would seem also that the more substantial constraints encountered in organization-building, such as staffing and money, do not allow for Publications as a priority.

Recruitment. This has been a major tactic for both NABSW and NAHSE as new, national organizations. While only the health administrators had significantly perceived Recruitment as a form of racism, both groups have sought to increase membership predominantly from current black practitioners and student bodies. While a great deal of Recruitment is conducted by local affiliates, both national bodies provided for student membership as a continuous source of recruits. Even though Recruitment ranked low among perceptions, it appears to rate high in tactics. This may be attributed to a strong sense of kinsmanship and closer interpersonal contact among persons of the same ethnic background.

Among the health administrators, Recruitment to the profession, to NAHSE, and to the white associations has been the major tactic for dealing with racism. Recruitment tactics involved the following: involve all minority group health administrators; locate via survey and enroll minority students from all professional schools; orient undergraduates for health careers; develop brochures, films, and other media for presentations at high schools and conferences; provide information on scholarships for graduate study.

Because of the scarcity of minority personnel in health administration, increased efforts toward increasing their numbers offers a concrete and tangible means of actively intervening in the racist health system. Concentration on Recruitment as a tactic must take cognizance of the nature of administration as a "producing and doing" activity. Because the health administrators as a group failed to question some of the substantial racist components in an organization such as Values, Coalition and Alliance, Publications, or Funding, their tactics would not be concentrated in these areas.

Conferences. Among white associations, Conferences have been indicators of racist patterns for both social workers and health administrators. The paucity of blacks in attendance, planning, panel participation, and published proceedings was obvious to black professionals. It might be inferred that Conferences would be a major tactical area for newly-formed black groups since Conferences are a primary means for organizing.

Both groups developed their own Conferences in order to deal with topics and issues more akin to their own special group interests. NABSW has held three national

conferences, usually during the week of Malcolm X's birth-
day—symbolic of the organization's emphasis on black
nationalism and on fostering self-determination.

NAHSE has had more national meetings than national
conferences. Its meetings have aimed at developing the
organization's internal operations. Its conferences usually
met in conjunction with the established white associations,
such as AHA, ACHA and AUPHA.

Although independent conferences have been convened,
various members and other conferees in both organizations
have often been in doubt as to whether their own finances
could permit their attendance. It would seem that there is
some question by employers and black professionals themselves as to the justification for these conferences.

Education and Training. As a manifestation of racism, this
ranked low among the perceptions of both social workers
and health administrators.

In NABSW, the tactics developed for Education and
Training were minor. There is no national, permanent
structure for education programs, college recruitment, career orientation, or scholarship assistance, as yet. In view
of the fact that social workers were a younger group, new
to the profession, and recent college graduates, it could be
inferred that Education and Training would be a more
active area.

It was just the opposite, however, for NAHSE. The fact
that so much of its program would be devoted to Education and Training may be attributed to these factors: first,
the leaders who actually perceived the racism may not be
the most active persons in terms of carrying out programs;
second, Education and Training may be the most feasible
route for program direction in view of the handicaps, such
as unpaid staff; third, Education and Training is also a

route toward compensating for the obvious lack of minority personnel in health management, and toward increasing the numerical strength of NAHSE; fourth, Education and Training seems to be a major concern among the health administrators because of their own upper-middle-income norms for mobility, progress, and status. For a group whose approaches emphasize integrating and working within the current health system, Education and Training provides a "safe" tactic, that is non-threatening to the establishment groups.

Coalition and Alliances. The efforts expended upon Coalition as a tactic for dealing with racism have been minimal among social workers in NABSW, even though they appeared to be more politically aware.

By contrast, the health administrators, have been much more active than the social workers in combining and integrating their efforts with most of the established, white, professional health associations. Characteristically, the health administrators appeared as a more moderate group, who are less identified with a strong black ideology. Recognizing the established groups as having both power and prestige, NAHSE has negotiated for resources and assistance. One of the problems which ensues from this cooperative venture is that most actions end up as programs or action by the parent group.

Some of the organizational constraints NAHSE faced, as a new organization with meager funds, no physical facilities, and no paid staff, moved this group to develop fewer "separate" approaches to its problems. However, on the whole, the black health administrators traditionally have been individuals who were "integrationists." They entered the system by being like whites. The older group seemed more inclined toward collaborative activities with white groups.

Funding. The tactics developed by NABSW for financing support of programs depended largely on membership dues, securing public funds, or special fund-raising activities. The latter have been aimed at securing money from the indigenous black community and little effort is directed toward private foundations. There is stronger adherence to the principle of black people supporting black institutions if these institutions are to become truly reflective of community control.

Among the health administrators, a more diversified view was taken in considering the financial support for NAHSE. Public funds and private foundations, as well as the corporate structure and membership dues, are relied upon for operation. The health administrators appear to be "doers" who are less identified with a values system which strongly emphasizes black, nationalistic trends. While NAHSE perceived their efforts as leading toward self-determination, self-help is achieved by creating and using any available resources to achieve its goals.

Staffing. Social workers have not engaged in an activity aimed at dealing with racism in the Staffing pattern of the white organization. Their efforts have been aimed, instead, at Staffing the NABSW and the local Chapters in the various cities.

While Staffing was highly perceived by both social workers and health administrators as a racist indicator, the health administrators have structured NAHSE to deal with white groups in contrast to NABSW. Illustrative of this was the establishment of a Joint Committee, inherent in NAHSE organizational structure, which would work with AHA. The American College of Hospital Administrators appointment of five NAHSE members to committees again reflects the effort for increased black participation in the staffing of the white association. [2]

Evaluation. Neither group of black professionals has developed tactics for dealing with Evaluation directly in order to lessen the racism perceived in that area in white associations. Perhaps they have assumed that the inclusion of more blacks in Programs, Conferences, and Staffing, especially as seen in the more incremental and integrative approaches by health administrators, automatically provides some solution to racist evaluative criteria and procedures of white groups.

As the more ethnic-based, "separate"-interest group with its own ties to a black values system, the social workers have striven to eliminate the racist elements in evaluative measures and procedures, countering with criteria that are reflective of black interests.

Organizational Values. Both groups of black professionals have tried to inculcate a recognition and promotion of black self-interest. In this way, each group sees itself as offering some measure of changing the traditional concept of professionalism. Despite the health administrators' lack of perception of racism in this category, they do see their organization as having some community service or consumer interest rather than as being merely a group of elitist, black professionals maintaining their own interests.

Because of the smaller number of health administrators, they have done less in terms of concrete programs and participation by consumers than the social workers.

The social workers are a more service-oriented group, whereas, by its nature, health administration is more concerned with executive and organizational functioning. While the latter has been concerned with the type of health services consumers receive, NAHSE tactics have not been concentrated as frequently in this area.

Scholarships and Awards. The social workers and health

administrators gave a low ranking to this area as an indicator of racism. NABSW has developed no formal program in Scholarships, Awards and Grants. There are indications that local Chapters have confronted various schools of social work regarding their available scholarships and policies in relation to minority students.

NAHSE, however, while not providing its own scholarships to students, has spearheaded the contribution of funds from various sources to AUPHA Work Study and Scholarship Loan Programs. NAHSE, in conducting its Recruitment programs, has contacted and stimulated the parent, white, professional associations for education in health administration to support these efforts. Their catalytic action was carried to private foundations, such as Kellogg and Weir.

NAHSE's emphasis on procuring Scholarships for blacks to prepare for health administration posts, thereby minimizing the present imbalance in minority representation, constitutes a major goal. It is one means of changing the white, established health institutions as well as developing leverage for its own organization. The emphasis on education is also reflective of its middle-class orientation and adherence to education and mobility in its values system.

Official Position on Social Issues. The social workers exerted the greater effort in the area of Official Positions in comparison with the health administrators, who had no frequent activity in this area. This might be expected in view of the fact that this younger, less assimilated, more ideological, and lower socio-economic group of social workers is more articulate and perceptive about institutional racist patterns. They perceived highly that one of the indicators of a white association's racism is its failure to speak out and protest on behalf of black people and black interests.

Even with such factors as being older, more assimilated, upper socio-economic, and apolitical, the health administrators also perceived highly this racist form but failed to exert much effort in this area. While the local New York Chapter has taken a number of positions on local health issues, the national organization's only major individual effort was reflected in the NAHSE position paper presented to the Congressional Black Caucus. But NAHSE also participated effectively in developing the AHA position of Health Care for the Disadvantaged. [3] Essentially, however, the NAHSE position was the AHA statement.

NOTES

1. Ernest Erber, *Urban Planning in Transition*, (New York: Grossman Publishers, 1970), p. 140.

2. Minutes, NAHSE Annual Meeting, Chicago, Ill., April 24, 1971, p. 2.

3. *Statement of Health Care for the Disadvantaged*, American Hospital Association, approved by House of Delegates, February 18, 1970.

10 | Comparing the Strategies of NABSW and NAHSE

WHILE THERE WERE AREAS in which both groups which we studied were taking action, their tactics were quite different for dealing with institutional racism. Consequently their strategies would also be different.

Strategies and Tactics. In our previous discussion regarding tactical areas, a definition was offered for the term "tactic." Strategy, constrastingly, considers the *overall, settled course of action.* Rein and Morris observed:

> ... a strategy involves a set of basic assumptions about a style of action judged most appropriate to accomplish specific aims. [1]

Although both strategy and tactics are instrumental, means-oriented, approaches to achieve specified organizational goals, strategy includes a more long-term plan of action predicated upon some theory of cause and effect. Tactics are the somewhat more constant methods of action. [2]

Essentially, then, the two organizations have developed different styles of implementing their tactics, although both of them are independent organizations. Their strategies are based on their distinctive social characteristics and perceptions of institutional racism, and the differing nature of their professions. The two styles can be contrasted to show how each group proceeded in its own way to achieve its specific aims.

The area of strategy and tactics is frequently dealt with in social science literature, especially in military science and community organization theory. In order to develop a conceptual framework for our analysis of the comparative strategies among social workers and health administrators, the areas of change, power, or conflict as aspects of organization theory are useful models. Rein and Morris offer some insights on strategies for change in their efforts to show the relationship between the goals, structures, and strategies employed by community organization practitioners. [3] It is their thesis that success in achieving a goal in community organization depends upon the use of a structure and a strategy appropriate to that goal; conversely no method however well implemented is effective in all circumstances. The authors also refer to goals of change and goals of integration. Certain strategies and structures must exist for obtaining these goals. Two different strategies which are termed as "cooperative rationality" and "individual rationality" are given. "Cooperative rationality" places a high premium on consensus; it seeks to set goals in which the majority of participants are in agreement. A major objective of this strategy is internal integration. "Individual rationality" refers to the predetermined, specialized, vested interests. It places greater stress on pluralistic values and on the inherent legitimacy of each unique and special objective. A strategy of individual rationality is best suited for goals of change, for new ideas where diversity or pluralism is encouraged. These then are factors to be considered in bringing about community change among distinctive, organizational structures such as simple or federated.

Collaboration, Campaigns, Contests. Three different types of purposive change have been suggested by Warren in reference to community problem solving. [4] These patterns are collaboration, campaigns, and contests. These types of change strategy are viewed in relation to issue situations. Collaboration strategies correspond to issue-agreement situations and are based on a common set of values and interests. Campaign strategies correspond to issue-difference situations and are based on a lack of agreement. In this case, a position is not shared, but there is the prospect of reaching an agreement. Contest strategies correspond to issue-*dissensus* situations. They are characterized by abandonment, temporarily at least, of efforts at consensus and the employment of efforts to further one's own side of an issue despite opposition from important parties to that issue.

From these discussions on types of strategies for change, we can see that strategies have been conceptualized in several different ways. Even though these two groups of black professionals used different approaches, we do find some overlap in their efforts to develop viable black professional organizations. This overlap creates some difficulty in clearly distinguishing the separate strategies of both groups. The strategies then are not pure or distinctive, because of the following factors: (1) both groups have grown up in a climate of strong, black militant protest, (2) each group is emerging under limited organizational resources; (3) the major target system is the black community, and not change in white established professional associations (although there will be side effects on white groups); (4) both groups symbolize regroupment rather than "separation" in the black community (it is not "separation" for any groups to come together on common policy); (5) both groups emphasize strategies related to functional objectives, that is, how the black condition is. It would be misleading to refer to these black professional associations' approaches as "integrationist" or "separationist," as the terms have come to cause considerable confusion. [5] When we view the strategies used by the emerging groups, we can see that the question of integration or separation is not germane to their approaches. But what is important is the type of actions and alternative systems which advance their cause and relieve the powerless and oppressive conditions for those blacks in the white, professional groups and the community at large.

With the emergence of these two black, professional associations, two strategies have been employed: the consolidative strategy and the collaborative strategy.

Consolidative Strategy. Used primarily by the social workers, the consolidative strategy refers to the more militant and assertive forces for achieving certain social and economic rights for black consciousness and subscribes to more of black nationalist ideology, wherein the development of "Black Power" gives attention to values and behavior. It is this element of the consolidative strategy which allowed the social workers to perceive many of the more covert forms of racism, such as Organizational Goals and Values, Role and Function, and Official Position. The consolidative strategy emphasizes community responsibility and accountability. This was also apparent in both groups' tactical areas, particularly in the social workers' emphasis on unifying a strong, black community. There is emphasis on the local community, rather than a unified mass movement. The policies, programs, and conditions of specific communities are the chief concerns. Underlying much of the consolidative approach is a relationship to political socialization of all African people. The members subscribed to the nationalistic ideology and issues related to the colonization of all black people. The principles of adherence to independence, self-determination, and accountability are strongly felt.

In this study, many of these trends allowed the social workers to be more perceptive politically and concerned with more substantive forms in building an organization. The social workers were more concerned with a strong black base and hence encouraged coalition-building among blacks, rather than developing white coalitions or alliances with the power structure. Social workers believe that the power structure in the professional association runs the system and is deeply involved in institutional racism.

The social workers' use of the consolidative strategy was illustrated also by their interest in the community, in terms of emphasizing consumer input in their programs, and the broad membership policies. For an example, one local chapter developed a neighborhood store front operation. This facility provides a continuous monitoring of needs and grievances, and provides additional inputs from community residents to the programs. This also brings a broader membership base, requiring fewer traditional credentials.

In reference to the solidarity of black people, the consolidative strategy is reflected in the social workers' endorsement of Official Positions, development of Program Activity, and Conferences built around such national concerns as Malcolm X Day, Black Power, and Black Solidarity Day throughout the black community. The social workers consider one of their primary goals the building of group power, which reinforces a kind of pride and heritage in blackness. The development of an annual Afro-American Day Parade, United Federation of Black Community Organizations by NABSW's New York chapter shows the principle of black integration and unity.

The employment of the consolidative strategy is congruent with the general social characteristics of the social workers. As a younger, activist group, more identified with a black ideology, with less vested interest in the profession and the professional associations, and with a willingness to perform leadership roles as organizers and implementers, the social workers could be expected to choose this approach for dealing with racism. Their perception of the forms of racism, particularly in the areas of Staffing, Program, Role and Function, Goals, and Values, are indices of the social workers' little faith in working with the white organizations. Consequently, the collaborative strategy would not be appropriate for them. With their degrees of perceptions of institutional racism, especially the covert forms, their trends toward pursuing more consolidative approaches could be inferred. The group, in essence, probably perceived this approach as more liberating, having more long-range benefits for strength and power in the black community.

Collaborative Strategy. Of the two main strategies among these black professional groups, the collaborative strategy was used primarily by the health administrators. The collaborative strategy refers to that course of action in which bargaining, confrontation, cooperation, and education were used as techniques. More joint committees and alliances are formed around common causes. Warren observed that in collaborative strategies there are mutual values and interests which provide for agreement on proposal or issues. [6] The predominant role of the change agent is that of an enabler or catalyst. The role of the health administrators has been chiefly that, particularly in their joint committee activities with the more established white groups. In the joint educational programs, NAHSE seemed to have stimulated new program activities for many of the established white groups.

Another illustration of the collaborative strategy, was the catalytic role of NAHSE's joint work with the AHA Joint Committee, and NAHSE's Education Committee's joint Summer Recruitment Program with the Association of University Programs in Hospital Administration. To further apply the collaborative strategy, NAHSE's Committee on Relations with the American College of Hospital Administrators, and the AHA support of NAHSE's establishment of national headquarters in the AHA headquarters are all examples of this newly-formed association's collaborative-coalitional efforts.

The health administrators, then, in terms of building their base in the black community, have chosen to deal in collaborative-coalitional efforts with many more white groups than the social workers. NAHSE is pursuing a reassignment of resources, change in status, and changes in the quality of health care to disadvantaged groups.

The use of this collaborative strategy correlates with the general social characteristics of the health administrators. As a group they were older and showed more vested interest in their jobs, the profession, and the white, health, professional associations. Their careers had developed at a time when integration was the main ethic underlying race relations.

The health administrators' perceptions of institutional racism are indicative of their style of strategy. They did not perceive racism with the degree of intensity, nor did they perceive many of the more substantial forms of racism. Consequently, they did not challenge the white structure, but chose to introduce more blacks into the health establishment. In view of the small numbers of minority personnel in health management, to them this was the most feasible approach. It would seem that if the goals and values of the parallel white groups were not questioned, then it is likely that an emerging interest group would work more closely within the existing structure. The fact that this group would choose the collaborative strategy as its main course was further reflected in their perception of racism. When interviewed, health administrators tended to be more protective and cautious in speaking about the white groups. In fact, the health administrators often referred to their health care delivery institution as the point of reference for racism rather than the white professional health association.

The collaborative strategy for health administrators presumably allows NAHSE to collaborate both with providers and with consumers. The newly established Health Consumers Accreditation Council of NAHSE is an integral part of planning and accrediting of hospitals', unions', and insurance companies' medical programs. It expresses NAHSE's collaborative strategy and its two-pronged objective to secure recognition of both black health consumers and black providers. While its program is responsive to the health needs of black people, its collaborative strategy represents an effort to work both within and outside of the black community. Perhaps the comment by one leader aptly describes the context of NAHSE's approach to racist patterns in the health system:

> Both black and white people get sick. Since blacks are informed as well as whites, the two must work together and have inputs from both sides. From the top level to the bottom level, inputs can be made which provide the type of care which is necessary for all people.

In general, then, the consolidative and collaborative

strategies can be summarized as follows: social workers tended to focus more within the black community for its ideology and resources, stressing the ideal of building and strengthening the community. To mirror the values inherent in the group's interests and ties with the community, social workers have based their efforts more broadly to encourage consumer input, informing policy and planning programs, as well as to develop a more diversified membership pattern.

Health administrators chose to deal more frequently with white, professional health associations through negotiations, confrontations, cooperative dialogues, and committees (such as the AHA Joint Committee), and appeals for money. While the health administrators have included in their values base a concern for consumers, they have done little to implement it in their relationships with the indigenous black community.

Despite the two dissimilar strategies we do see similar achievements for both groups. They have become spokesmen, have provided alternatives in certain tactical areas, and have stimulated changes in the traditional white associations. Each of the groups is providing services to its membership. In the case of NABSW, more services are offered to the consumers as well. A communication system has at least been established among blacks in the profession. This is the beginning of developing some operational unity, which is a long-range matter. The national conferences are also a mechanism for this communication system. It is at these conferences that national goals and priorities for the health and social service aspects of the black community have been reached. Each group is trying to build and assess the strengths and values of the black community. Consequently, the black professionals' main preoccupation has been aimed at developing organizational structure among these groups. This long-range process has necessitated a reorientation and education for both blacks and whites. At the same time a minimum amount of services has been offered. Indeed, black professional social workers and health administrators have actually been the real protagonists of the white racist social welfare and health professional associations.

An analysis of the current strategies of NABSW and NAHSE is also related to their earlier history in which both associations initially developed similar approaches to race relations in professional associations. As time passed, the social workers, however, converted to the consolidative approach. Some discussion of the initial strategies will provide an overview of what was to become the major courses of action for these groups.

NABSW's Initial Strategies. Although the social workers saw the establishment of independent organizations as the major strategy, historically there have been initial strategies among the earlier black social work leaders to deal openly with at least one of the predominantly white, established, social work organizations during the 1968 and 1969 NCSW Forums. Prunty reported that in 1968 the NABSW was one of three organizations that attempted to radicalize the conference by requesting that it embrace a broader spectrum of activities rather than be simply a "forum." NABSW, subsequently, set up its separate conference. [7]

During the 1969 NCSW Forum, the NABSW formed a loose coalition consisting of the National Welfare Rights Organization, Organization of Spanish-Speaking Social Workers, and the Women of America Revolution. These groups occupied the platform of the opening session, against insisting that NCSW become more than a convener of an educational forum. NABSW also backed the demands made by NWRO, that the NCSW contribute $35,000 to finance NWRO work. The NCSW National Board voted to appropriate this amount and to pay expenses of 250 NWRO members to attend the 1970 Forum.

While a variety of other protest groups made demands on NCSW, the NABSW demanded that black individuals participate in policy making. Consistent with their perception of racism in the Staffing pattern of predominantly white groups, a 50 percent representation of blacks and brown people on the Board, staff and program committees of NCSW was requested. A lobbyist in Washington was also requested who would work with black organizations to influence national welfare policies and legislation. There was a call for NCSW and CSWE to develop more relevant educational curricula and provide blacks with a stronger role in admissions policies, financial aid programs, and faculty appointments. [8]

These demands were endorsed and supported by NCSW, although the level of changes was higher among conference attendees than among NCSW officialdom. An Implementation Committee consisting of NABSW and NCSW members was innovated to provide for continuity in the hearing of minority demands.

NABSW's mode of direct intervention with this one established, white professional organization represented their most extensive tactic for dealing with racism in white groups. The group's use of disruptive tactics was aimed at preventing the system from continuing "business as usual." As to these initial strategies, Prunty observed:

> These strategies and tactics were nonviolent but they were utilized only after all other remedies had been exhausted. Furthermore, they were utilized with an awareness of the consequences. The question as to what disruptive tactics were utilized is a real anachronism. The more logical question is why

> such groups have been forced to go to such ex-
> tremes to be heard and to force the system to alter
> its institutions radically and to remove those legal,
> educational, and social roadblocks that have been
> destructive to black family life and degrading to
> their personalities. [9]

These developments tend to show that there has been an emerging process on the part of NABSW to deal with racism. March and Simon suggest four strategies for dealing with institutional change. These are: problem solving, education and persuasion, negotiation and bargaining, and use of pressure. [10] During the first year, NABSW made use of all of these, including alliance tactics. During the first year, as a major white establishment was confronted, disorder and tensions were fluid.

The fact that leadership has changed might cause one to overlook these initial NABSW strategies. As the organization pushed forward, there was less effort toward confronting white groups with the interest of change. The tendency has been to turn inward, reflecting the black nationalist emphasis on colonization, land, self-determination, and accountability as the basic elements. [11] Consequently, the newer leadership among the social workers developed their strategy toward building a separate black organization.

NAHSE's Initial Strategies. From the beginning of its early informal meeting in November 1967, NAHSE was envisioned as a separate, ethnic-based, professional health association, consisting primarily of minority group personnel in various decision-making positions in the medical and health field. During the initial meeting in New York, this predominantly black group felt the need to exchange the common problems which they found in the health establishment.

After a series of monthly meetings, the group decided to establish a permanent organization. They saw as their initial purposes: (1) the identification of black and other minority group personnel in the health field; (2) the identification of plans and devices for solving on-the-job problems; (3) the recruitment of black and Puerto Rican personnel into health services administration; and (4) the promotion of group solidarity to encourage social and fraternal relationships within the association.

Efforts to develop and expand into a national program were initiated by the New York group at the 70th National Meeting of the American Hospital Association in Atlantic City, New Jersey in September 1968. The black health executives held a caucus and those attending were generally impressed with the activities of the New York group. There was, however, conflict around the need for an ethnic basis of membership for such an organization. In spite of the conflict, the black organization emerged at this predominantly white AHA convention for the following possible reasons: (1) the impact of the conducive climate for black activism; (2) the common alienation and powerlessness encountered by the smattering of blacks in health management positions; and, (3) the obvious plight and awareness of the poor health conditions in black America.

In essence, the strategy was to develop NAHSE as a separate, independent group. It was not an in-house protest group for AHA, but merely used the established white association's conference as a convenient meeting place for organizing minority personnel, since this was a well-known, well-attended, annual, professional meeting. From the outset NAHSE recognized that some of its members would participate in AHA, ACHA, and AUPHA, but their representation would be as members of these groups. But, in other instances, NAHSE is represented in its own right. From its initial stages, NAHSE has collaborated with established, white professional health associations. For example, the Joint Committee of the two associations for dealing with policy-making of hospitals on all levels is one of the joint efforts. There has also been collaboration on AHA Council of Approved Schools of Hospital Administration.

This early history simply reflects NAHSE's beginning approach as one in which the organization utilized a coalitional, cooperative approach in working with the non-black groups.

NOTES

1. Martin Rein and Robert Morris, "Goals, Structures, and Strategies for Community Change," *Social Work Practice*, (New York: Columbia University Press, 1962).

2. Harry Specht, "Disruptive Tactics," *Social Work*, Vol. 14, No. 2, (April 1969), pp. 5-15.

3. Martin Rein and Robert Morris, *op. cit.*, pp. 127-45.

4. Roland Warren, "Types of Purposive Social Change at the Community Level," in *Readings in Community Organization Practice*, ed. by Ralph M. Kramer and Harry Specht, (Englewood Cliffs, N.J.: Prentice-Hall, Inc., 1969).

5. Lerone Bennett, Jr., "Liberation," *Ebony*, Vol. XXV, No. 10, (August 1970), pp. 36-45.

6. Warren, *op. cit.*, p. 210.

7. Prunty, *op. cit.*, pp. 185-192.

8. Association of Black Social Workers, Position Statement, National Conference on Social Welfare, New York, May 20, 1969. (Unpublished.)

9. Prunty, *op. cit.*, p. 183.

10. March and Simon, *op. cit.*, pp. 129-130.

11. Herman Blake, "Black Nationalism," *The Annals*, 382, (March 1969), p. 24.

11 | Implications for Future Action by All Black Professional Organizations

LEADERS OF ALL BLACK PROFESSIONAL SOCI-
ETIES will find implications here for the future directions
of their organizations—implications now even more important since at least twenty such groups have emerged during
the past six years. In assessing the societal matrix from
which NABSW and NAHSE emerged, our study has revealed these germinal components, equally relevant to the
newer, emerging groups:

1. Black professional organizations thrive when
   there is protest. The health administrators had
   been organized previously to NAHSE's formation. However, it was the protest in the sixties
   that crystallized the issues and clarified the actions needed for reducing the alienation and
   powerlessness of black health administrators.

2. Black professional organizations thrive when
   there is identification with a black values system. The increasing cultural nationalism, revealed as black consciousness, provided potency
   and vigor to the development of black organizations.

3. Black professional organizations thrive when the white established institutions are unresponsive to the interests and needs of the powerless and alienated black segment of their membership. This was especially consistent with the experience of the health administrators who had initiated an organization in early 1940. [1]

In discussing the future directions of black professional groups, it is important to explain the difference between the white perspective and the black perspective. Our discussion of future directions is placed within the context of the black perspective, that the development of new institutions in the black community parallels issues in developmental administration or community development. [2] The problems and resources for building new institutions and organizations in the black community are similar to those encountered by developing nations. Therefore, any projections or assessments must be cautiously made, in that evaluative criteria must not be gauged solely on established white institutional standards.

The future directions of emerging black professional groups must be considered within this context. If white, established institutions had been more responsive to the needs of clients and professionals, then these black groups might not have developed. Realizing that integration had not fully developed, these groups became a manifestation that political strength, cohesion and ability to exert pressure and influence in a society come through organized special interest groups.

Long Range Goals. It is apparent to the more militant and assertive black professional that established institutions may increase the number of blacks and other minority persons through Recruitment, but that there will still be the need for organizations in the black community. Consequently, with this ideology, we will see more and more groups developing, but the pathos and militancy surrounding the formation of these new groups will have to be viewed in terms of resources for implementation and programmatic goals.

Institutionalization. The issue of viability is imminent as future actions are envisioned for these groups. What are the prospects of each group's viability? Although both NABSW and NAHSE have made substantial programmatic, organizational, and intrinsic achievements, projections of their future performance are needed. It is obvious that unless both find financial resources other than in their membership base, their activities may wane. Each organization's viability is questionable unless basic strategies are developed for funding, whether by private donors or public funds. Some of the current, voluntary staff has devoted the time and creativity for developing sound programs, but those are not enough to sustain the organization's national offices with paid staff. There has been a strong feeling among the social workers that funding resources exist in the black community. Building an institutional base on poor and lower-middle-income levels will not yield the necessary results. The financial base for these organizations is not entirely in the black community. Blacks have also contributed to the public subsidies. Even the established, white traditional institutions, such as NASW and CSWE, during these strained economic times, are having trouble surviving. The question, then, is how can emerging black groups sustain themselves when their thrust for independence has come during one of the most repressive periods in history? It would seem that these organizations must set up programs aimed at securing public subsidies like many of the other ethnic-based organizations in this country.

While it has been asserted that the financial means for sustenance and determination of the black community exists within the community, these resources have not been accessible. A resource base built solely on the black community will take a longer period of time. In the meantime, the question of organizational survival is raised for these organizations. Are they to be organizations with all the trimmings of the established, white, professional associations with national conferences, publications, etc?

Unless a stronger resource base is developed, none of these groups can be molders of structural change. Currently they are keeping issues visible and are spokesmen. They have provided alternatives, but their functions need to be solidified on a more permanent basis.

Newly-formed, black professional groups have provided a source of stimulation and force to the "people's movement." They offer a great deal of support to other community interest groups, technical assistance to other organizations, and a role model for black children.

In view of the marginal existence of some of the groups, it would also seem that a national federation of black professional organizations might be considered among the various disciplines and professions. There would probably be strains amidst various vested interests, but the formation of such an organization would maximize contributions to the struggle for black liberation. In this study, there are serious implications that the future direction for black professionals must involve building stronger coalitions among themselves, which will help to give clarity to a strong black base.

The penetrating examples of ingrained institutional racism shown in the study underline need for the socialization process of continuing to change the perceptions of whites. But this should not be a priority. More importantly, the framework within which their problems and the black professional are defined, must be continuously examined. Future directions for black professionals might include coalition with radical whites, as well as other minority and ethnic groups. Stronger bases can be built with some of these allies who have some of the same problems and common interests.

From this study, both social work and health professional organizations show that their strategy evolved from expediency and, in some instances, uncoordinated tactics. Both groups should remain mindful that they emerged because of problems with blackness. Their main agenda, values, and programs must mirror the need from which they originated. As national emerging organizations, both NABSW and NAHSE will need clarity of goals, talent, group cohesion, knowledge, skill and finances. A continuous eye on the racist health and social welfare system can serve as a monitor for program activity. Both groups will need to project long-range plans which must be analyzed as to possibilities for failure or success. Because the patterns of institutional racism are pervasive in health and social welfare institutions, each organization must cautiously arrange its system of priorities and move with deliberate action.

NOTES

1. Files of Huston Baker, Director of Freedmen's Medical Center, Washington, D.C. See: Notes on the National Conference of Hospital Administrators.

2. Gabriel A. Almond and James S. Coleman, *The Politics of the Developing Areas,* (Princeton, N.J.: Princeton University Press, 1960).

12 | Implications for Public Administration

This study, although it does not deal primarily with a public institution, is particularly relevant to public administration. The study of black professionals' perceptions of institutional racism in established, white professional associations is a revealing aspect of the increasing self-consciousness and increasing alienation that middle-level blacks in service professions were experiencing. Their situation of powerlessness was more imminent when the thrust for power and accountability became more visible throughout the country. Many of the findings and conclusions can help provide guidelines for change in the public service institutions in which these professions are found. Because of these black professionals' challenges to the establishment, the associations and service institutions can become more responsive to the needs of any relatively "disadvantaged" group.

This study has many implications for the administrative process in general because it deals with the socio-political context of a social movement acting upon established institutions as well as with the creation of new institutions. The implications of the findings in this study are applicable to both the study and practice of public administration. The implications can be viewed within at least three contexts. One aspect is the role of social environmental factors (protest and racist patterns) in the administrative setting. Based upon these protest issues a new kind of administrative practice, referred to as "advocacy administration," has appeared. The next context of this study's implications is that of public personnel. Aspects of organizational development are discussed as the final area of implications.

It was obvious from this study that both social work and health management as public service occupations were in dire need of reform of some of their professional practices. Both social workers and health administrators have played a role in having both the black and white community examine their professional responsibilities. A new kind of professionalism developed, particularly when both groups equated their plight with their responsibility to their black clients. Because the client system is changing in so many of the large, inner-city, bureaucratic complexes, it has raised new issues of policy making, types of services, and employment patterns for the public administrator. The traditional "elitist professionalism," whereby membership interests and standards often outweighed the emphasis on consumers of service, has been seriously challenged.

These black professionals have politicized administration in the sense that the administrator must respond to these issues. The development of advocacy in public administration will take on greater significance in the future. [1] This new concern will tell us that public organizations must seek ways to become more representative of constituent desires. The tactical areas of Goals and Values among both social workers and health administrators reflected their expressed concern with these issues.

These black professional groups have moved their institutions much closer to considering the needs and interests of their membership, as well as advocating that the white institution get involved with contemporary domestic and social issues. The issues of advocacy administration have been centrally focused for the black institutions, which blacks are developing, and for the established white institutions, if they are to change. Black professionals in these two professions, which are found primarily in the public sector, have posed such questions as: Will blacks have a chance to participate in policy-making decisions? Will blacks have more opportunities in these professions?

The black professional was asking the white organizations: Who are we? What do we believe? He was indeed a force contending for dominance. The black professionals gave themselves and established white professional associations a chance for re-evaluation and assessment. These black professionals have created a more open system as a result of their protest. In essence they were allowing the white association to really move further toward their ideals and credence in equality and democratic participation. With the black professional contribution to a new kind of professionalism, the administrative structure of the established, white institutions has had to change. The blacks were calling for change and innovation in administrative systems—change that could only come through reexamination of both the black and white groups' values, goals, and reasons for existence. The black professionals, in another way, were saying to white institutions, "Get involved—there is a social revolution going on in this country." This means that the white, professional association had to find ways of adapting to these environmental changes. Some did, by "blackenizing" their associations. From the social workers' protest we saw the administrative changes made by NASW. For example, their consciousness of the problem lead to inclusion of more minority staff; publications dealing with minority content; and a statement on racism. With the white health professional association, we saw the inclusion of more blacks on the national staff, joint committees, and cooperative projects with NAHSE.

Advocacy administration has meant that the newly-emerging black groups were also adapting to the change in the black community, reflecting its new mood and theme. The theme indicated a thrust for more black control and self-determination which, in turn, meant the creation of new institutions.

This study has a sensitizing role, in that it cautions administrators about the inequities, lack of opportunities, and repression in institutions. Although the black professional perceived forms of racism in the established, white professional associations, some of the same overt and covert forms of racism exist in service institutions. In any organization there are patterns of staffing, conferences, membership, official position, education and training, recruitment, and funding. Too often organizations are referred to as merely "racist organizations." This research documented authentic accounts of groups of alienated black professionals' perceptions of racist practices. The concrete conceptions of indicators of racism as shown by the frequency scale should be useful in developing a consciousness of how racism may manifest itself in any organization. The skilled administrator needs to be sensitive to these practices and conditions.

Within the field of public administration, the same attention placed on minority clients can be placed on minority professional personnel. White observed that one of the basic problems in public administration is its bureaucratic diagnosis when clients do not define their needs. [2] Miller and Rein complemented this concern when they observed that participatory demands of the poor have affected at least four areas of public administration—personnel, professional discretion, policy development, and accountability. [3] Within the context of public bureaucracy, the black professional would certainly have the same effect. The public agency which employs social workers and health administrators must not only examine its personnel practices and the participation of minorities in its formulations and development of policy, but also its accountability to other minority workers.

Of special relevance to public administration is the fact that these black groups have tested one of the most important constructs of the democratic system, the right and obligation of people to express their opinion. This is one of the cornerstones of the field and practice of American public administration. Indeed the words dissidence, conflict, radicalism, demonstration, protest, revolution, reform, representativeness, and maximum feasible participation were frequently echoed during the sixties by many minority groups other than black professionals. Equal opportunities, shared power, and participatory decision-making were also themes which highlighted the moods and preoccupations of the times. Boskin and Rosenstone noted:

> The dissidents of the 1960's have performed a service by questioning the values, assumptions and institutions of American society. Indeed they have gone further by proposing alternative programs for existing programs (as was indicated by black professionals). Such actions are necessary for the viability of the democratic state. . . . The overriding aim of the protesting groups has been their quest for a society in which the individual, regardless of race, age, class, and political persuasion, will be able to share in the democratic process. That to achieve this, it has become necessary for portions of society to organize and express themselves openly, and to risk injury and life, demonstrates how far America has fallen short of its promise. By

their words and actions the protestors have helped to remind us again of the gap between the reality and expectations of American life. [4]

This is simply one explanation of the dynamics of the black professional movement as they relate to American principles and ideals surrounding established institutions. To bring the problem closer to home, issues of protest and dissent are more acute for the administrators, particularly within the framework of large, public bureaucracies. The unrest experienced by many interest groups has become more vehement in the explosive 70's, as social conditions and scarce resources worsen in many of the inner-cities of the American metropolis. Administrators continue to rise to the occasion when protest groups demand a louder voice and greater share in planning, implementing, and gaining more goods and services from the American dream. All institutional and organizational settings over the next years will seriously and openly make more demands on administrators for some kind of institutional change.

This study of black professionals' dissent and reasons for forming their own organizations has relevance to public personnel practices, especially in the areas of Recruitment, Education and Training, Evaluation, and incentives. Through the exposure of institutional racist practices, public administrators can be sensitized to demands for job opportunities and to manpower resources, which heretofore have been invisible. Recruitment personnel in the area of social work and health management can develop more effective recruitment devices and training aids for attracting a greater percentage of minority personnel to careers in the field of health management and social work. The new community groups can be useful as contacts in recruiting personnel. Because of the black professionals' protest in recent times, a more assertive effort can be made to increase the participation of blacks, not only in jobs, but also on boards, commissions, and in other policy-making functions.

Public personnel administration, particularly within the framework of the United States Civil Service Commission, recognized its role in social progress during the 1960's. It is within the new directions of this agency's creation and utilization of fresh sources of manpower that this study can have major implications. From our study we have seen that black professionals have experienced disadvantages, and have felt alienated and left out of their professional association. They have "wanted in," and this trend carries over to employment opportunities.State and local governments are far short of black professional social work and health management personnel. This problem will continue to multiply as the job market continues to move toward service professions and organizations. Public personnel practices will have a major stake in improving the status of black professionals through recruitment, provision of educational opportunities, and employment career patterns.

An analysis of this research reveals the significance of perceptions and various actions for development of totally new and independent organizations in the black community. The roles of the leadership and their perceptions all help to determine the kinds of strategies and tactics for effecting change and innovation in an organization. In building a new organization, it is apparent that values, goals, external resources such as facilities, finances, and staff are crucial to organizational effectiveness. As we view the organizational process of these emerging organizations, we have been able to see the politico-psycho-social aspects of the black professionals' quest for identity and community development. Underlying much of the organizational activity are the efforts to lessen alienation and powerlessness, and the need for creating responsive institutions in the black community.

Hopefully, this study will provide knowledge to private and public administrators on the use of creative protest and conflict which can be useful in developing meaningful responses and accountability in their own institutions.

NOTES

1. H. George Frederickson, "Organization Theory and the New Public Administration," Maxwell School of Public Affairs, Syracuse University, 1969, (unpublished paper). Richard S. Page, "A New Public Administration?", *Public Administration Review*, May/June, 1969, Vol. XXIX, No. 3, p. 303.

2. Orion White, "The Dialectical Organization: An Alternative to Bureaucracy," *Public Administration Review*, (January/February 1969), p. 82.

3. S. M. Miller and Martin Rein, "Participation, Poverty, and Administration," *Public Administration Review*, (January/February 1969), pp. 18-19.

4. Boskin and Rosenstone, *op. cit.*, p. x.

Appendix

CASE STUDY: NATIONAL CONFERENCE OF
BLACK POLITICAL SCIENTISTS

Preliminary Findings

These are the findings on a pre-test of five leaders in the NCBPS, a
newly-formed professional association. Efforts were made to secure
their responses to three questions under study:

1. What do they perceive as forms of institutional racism in
   the established group?

2. What is their new organization doing about the racism?

3. How effective is their organization in dealing with the
   racism?

Manifestations of Racism

Among the respondents interviewed on this subject, each perceived a
pattern of racism in the areas of Staffing, Membership, Publications,
and Official Positions on Social Issues of the established, white
organizations. These respondents felt that these most frequent indicators of racism existed for a long time.

187

Staffing

One respondent typified many reactions in this area when he stated:

> The Staffing pattern, especially as viewed in board, chairmanship of committees, staff leaders, and consultants, reflected no blacks or other minority persons prior to 1967. There seems to have been apathy toward the blacks in this national association. . . I received a secret ballot from the national association in order to vote for Vice President, and you see all these white cats' names on the ballots; you start wondering and say what relevance is this to me? . . . I'm sure that there are some black political scientists who can serve on some of these important known committees. I don't think there are many instances where these white cats in main positions get to know any black people. . . . So once in awhile they may run across somebody that everybody knows, and they might suggest his name which means if he gets in, it is only a token base!

Another interviewee observed in relation to an obvious racist pattern among the leadership:

> The association, even at the behest of pressures brought on by blacks in the profession has not listed any blacks for nomination to the committee structure, even though a roster of candidates was suggested by the Committee on the Status of Blacks. Blacks in decision-making positions have been non-existent, and consequently our interests have not been represented.

Membership

Membership, as one of the most frequently perceived racist indicators in the established white organization, was observed in the following statement:

> When the association is interested in all persons with Ph.D.'s and established reputations and scholars, how can this come about if the system does not provide opportunity for money and degrees?

Publications

This dimension of racism in the organization was most frequently perceived as the lack of black members on editorial boards, publication staff, and the lack of black authors of articles, as well as black content material in the publications. According to one black professor:

> The reason we don't get in the literature is because the predominance of black political scientists are so busy in the classrooms of predominantly black colleges, teaching!

Another respondent noted that his profession's national journal had accepted only six articles of black authors, since its origin in 1905!

> This is an obvious example of racism which has something to do with values. . . . The standards that get things published are always *my* meeting particular standards. . . I think black people have to set their own standards as to what is competence and confidence in his particular field. Name any outstanding black in whatever field and he is a political writer. Blacks are going to have to set their own standards. For example: How many blacks ask themselves how long would some of these outstanding political scientists last if they were teaching twelve hours at Morehouse like I am. Most are teaching only a six-hour load.

In response to publications as a vehicle of racism in the established organization, another interviewee noted:

> Six years ago I submitted a manuscript on the black self-image which was rejected by several journals. We have been isolated commercially in terms of acceptance of our manuscripts. In a sense, even now blacks are being used commercially, so that people can make money, since black studies programs are in vogue.

Official Positions on Social Issues

The failure of the established, white, professional group to take a stance on social issues relevant to black people was the final most frequent perception of institutional racism. This pattern may be referred to as "administrative neutrality." One respondent observed:

> This professional organization has failed to adopt a position about racism in this country. The association refuses to go on record as saying it is opposed to racism, because it does not want to "impose" attitudes on its members. The association sees its role as a strictly "objective, academic, scholarly association." The most fundamental aspect of the organization is its commitment to a policy which would allow the publication, staffing, scholarships and membership patterns to fall into line.

Ideology; Conferences; Scholarships and Awards. The second most frequent range of perceptions of racist patterns among the sample group included the categories of Ideology, Conferences, and Scholarships, and Awards. By Ideology is meant the ways of thinking, or dominant opinions in the organization. This demension is closely related also to Organizational Values.

One respondent, who is a professor at a Southern black college, made the following comment regarding his professional organization:

> The standards and values of the organization has nothing to do with my values system; it is my meeting their particular standards.

It was noted that, among the American Political Science Association, an almost nonexistent number of blacks were in this profession. Scholarships for black students were nonexistent in political science. Since most persons saw the only opportunities for political scientists in college teaching, Recruitment for blacks in the profession consequently was also nonexistent. The Recruitment for the few black political scientists to college posts was even more restricted. One professor observed:

> Blacks certainly did not benefit from the resources of the professional association. . . . The Public Service Awards, in which newspapermen across the country receive awards, has never included the black press or black newsmen. . . The association's program for Congressional Fellow has also been out of the reach of black political scientists.

These perceptions of the pattern of non-recruitment of blacks can be borne out by the fact that the American Political Science Association, through its Committee on the Status of Blacks, initiated in September 1970, a program for Graduate Fellowships for black students. The 1971-72 program sought "to identify and aid blacks pursuing graduate study in political science." It offered 15 fellowships to outstanding applicants, as well as five one-year, $3,600 stipends to the top applicants. [1]

In the categories of Program Activity, Recruitment, Funding Source, Curriculum, Values, Policies and Interpersonal Relations, only one respondent perceived one of these organizational dimensions as a racist indicator in the professional association. The areas were not only those in which the subjects were aware of racism, but, in some instances, also areas in which they have experienced or encountered racism.

Of special significance in the pre-test group was the fact that none of the subjects perceived patterns of racism in the areas of Role and Function, Goals, and Coalitions.

Strategies for Dealing With Racism

Publications and Conferences

Among the respondents who were interviewed, the most frequent range of strategies for dealing with the forms of racism in the established white associations fell within the areas of Publications and Conferences. [2]

One might expect these efforts in view of the fact that the NCBPS is a newly-formed group. Conferences, where members can develop dialogue and exchange ideas about conditions, is the initial stage in organizational development. Publications, which consist of the discussion and writing of papers, is an integral part of the initial process of NCBPS. One professor, considering the beginning of this new group, said:

> We have to gain an awareness of our own needs; pool our resources, identify our talents as a unit as opposed to being disbursed throughout the association. In this emerging process, the organizational ideology is surpassed by two schools

of thought: there are those who talk about "separation" and "liberation," at the same time.

As a beginning organization, the topics chosen for discussion reflect the emerging or developing stage of the organization. For example, such areas as "Political Socialization of Black Children and Adults," and, "Role of the Black Political Scientist in the Black Community," were among the topics at the first annual conference. [3]

The conferences are allowing blacks to have input into research and curriculum. [4] One of the national leaders observed:

> As black political scientists we can start with our own experiences, as it is just natural if one were teaching in France or Russia to begin with the French or Russian experience.

In relation to Publications as a strategical area for dealing with racism, NCBPS has established a bi-monthly newsletter and a *Journal of Black Politics*. [5] Through such publications, the black experience in the political arena might be reflected more frequently and accurately.

Ideology, Coalitions and Official Positions

The second most frequent range of strategies in which NCBPS has dealt with the racist patterns included the organizational dimensions of Ideology, Coalitions, and Official Positions. The development of a definite ideology is an on-going process. One of the national leaders commented that

> the organizational concept for an oppressed people is their *oppression*. . . If people organize around that oppression and if people organize because of their race, it's only logical that they will organize. . . It's really not an organization around race, except for the fact that people have been oppressed as a race. For that reason it is necessary for African people to organize themselves *wherever* they are in whatever capacity they use their talents.

Effectiveness in Dealing With Racism

The majority of the subjects felt that NCBPS had not been as effective as it could have been. But due to the various organizational constraints, such as being understaffed and a voluntary professional association, much had been accomplished during the two-year period. It was indicated in the discussion of strategies to deal with racism, NCBPS, as an identifiable group with its on-going activities of an annual conference, publications, and education, gave some black political scientists a new sense of self-concept and made new strides. One leader noted that

> NCBPS has its own prospectus about what should be taught and how it should be taught. We are not a protest organization but a group of political scientists doing what it believes political scientists should be doing.

Another leader stated:

> Basically all we have is our ideology---no funds, no staff to carry on goals. Our volunteer workers are already overworked. I think this strains the organization. Our situation is almost comparable to the paraplegic. . .

Summary

Based upon these findings in the preliminary study, we were able to refine and extend the number of categories within the original frequency scale of institutional racist patterns. The final classification scheme was revised from the results of the pre-test with this similar black professional group with guidance from a research consultant, having extensive experience.

NOTES

1. "Political Science Association Offers Aid to Blacks," *Jet Magazine,* January 30, 1971, p. 4.

2. Position Paper: Black Caucus, *American Political Science Association*, September 1969. (Mimeographed) Lenneal Henderson, "Engineers for Liberation," *Black Politician*, April 1970.

3. Brochure: First Annual Conference, National Conference of Black Political Scientists, May 1970, Atlanta University, Atlanta, Ga.

4. Second Annual Conference, National Conference of Black Political Scientists, Howard University, Washington, D.C., May, 1971.

5. *Newsletter*, NCBPS, Atlanta University, Department of Political Science, Atlanta, Ga. 30314 (September 1971).

BIBLIOGRAPHY

Books

Almond, Gabriel A. and Coleman, James S., eds. *The Politics of the Developing Areas*. Princeton, N.J.: Princeton University Press, 1960.

Bartholomew, Paul C. *Public Administration*. Paterson, N.J.: Littlefield, Adams and Co., 1962.

Berelson, Bernard and Steiner, Gary A. *Human Behavior: An Inventory of Scientific Findings*. New York: Harcourt, Brace and World, Inc., 1964.

Blau, Peter M., and Scott, Richard. *Formal Organizations: A Comparative Approach*. San Francisco: Chandler Publishing Co., 1962.

Bogardus, Emory S. *Leaders and Leadership*. New York: Appleton-Century Co., 1934.

Carmichael, Stokely and Hamilton, Charles V. *Black Power: The Politics of Liberation in America*. New York: Vintage Books, 1967.

Craig, Colgate, Jr., ed. *1970 Directory of National Trade and Professional Associations of the United States*. Washington, D.C.: Columbia Books, Inc.

Daniels, Roger. *American Racism*. Englewood Cliffs, N.J.: Prentice-Hall, 1970.

Darbin, Richard L. *Organization and Administration of Health Care: Theory, Practice, and Environment*. Saint Louis: C. V. Mosby, 1969.

Edwards, G. Franklin. *The Negro Professional Class*. Glencoe, Ill.: Free Press, 1969.

Erber, Ernest. *Urban Planning in Transition.* New York: Grossman Publishers, 1970.

Etzioni, Amitai. *Modern Organizations.* Englewood Cliffs, N.J.: Prentice-Hall, 1964.

Hamilton, Charles V. "Black Militancy." In *New York Times Encyclopedic Almanac.* (New York: Quadrangle Books, 1970), pp. 307-8.

Hernton, Calvin C. *Sex and Racism in America.* New York: Grove Press, Inc., 1965.

Key, V. O. *Politics, Parties, and Pressure Groups.* 5th ed. New York: Crowell Co., 1964.

Kidneigh, John C. "The New York Conference Story." In *Social Welfare Forum, 1969.* New York: Columbia University Press, 1969.

Killingsworth, Charles. "Jobs and Income for Negroes." In *Race and Social Sciences,* Katz, Irwin, and Gurin, Patricia, eds. New York: Basic Books, 1969.

Kilpatrick, Franklin P., Cummings, Milton C., Jr., and Jennings, M. Kent. *Source Book of a Study of Occupational Values and the Image of the Federal Service.* Washington, D.C.: Brookings Institution, 1964.

Klein, Roger, ed. *The Profession of Hospital Administration.* Atlanta: Georgia Hospital Association, 1960.

Knowles, Louis L., and Prewitt, Kenneth. *Institutional Racism in America.* Englewood Cliffs, N.J.: Prentice-Hall, 1969.

Lipset, Seymour. *Political Man.* New York: Doubleday and Co., Inc., 1960.

——. *The First New Nation.* New York: Anchor Books, 1962.

Lowry, Louis. *Training Manual for Human Service.* New York: Harper and Row, 1962.

McGibony, John R. *Principles of Hospital Administration.* 2nd ed. New York: G. P. Putnam's Sons, 1969.

Malinowski, Bronisaw. *A Scientific Theory of Culture and Other Essays.* Chapel Hill: University of North Carolina Press, 1944.

March, James G., ed. *Handbook of Organizations.* Chicago: Rand McNally and Co., 1965.

March, James G., and Simon, Herbert A. *Organizations.* New York: John Wiley and Sons, Inc., 1961.

Meirer, August, and Rudwick, Elliott, eds. *Black -Protest in the Sixties.* New York: Quadrangle Books, 1970.

Merton, Robert K. *Social Theory and Social Structure*. New York: Free Press, 1957.

Morais, Herbert M. "Medicine and Health." In *Black America*, Romero, Patricia W., ed. Washington, D.C.: Association for the Study of Negro Life and History, 1969.

Murphy, Gardner. *Personality*. New York: Harper and Sons, 1947.

Numan, Louise, editor. *Service Directory of National Organizations*. New York: National Assembly for Social Policy and Development, Inc., 1969.

O'Reilly, Charles T. "Race in Social Welfare." In *Race, Research and Reason*. New York: National Association of Social Workers, 1969.

Pfiffner, John M., and Presthus, Robert V. *Public Administration*. 5th ed. New York: Ronald Press Co., 1967.

Presthus, Robert V. *The Organizational Society*. New York: Vintage Books, 1962.

Prunty, Howard E. "The New York Story—A Participant's Viewpoint." In *Social Welfare Forum, 1969*. New York: Columbia University Press, 1969.

Rein, Martin and Morris, Robert. "Goals, Structures and Strategies for Community Change," in *Social Work Practice*. New York: Columbia University Press, 1962.

Rosenberg, M. et al. *Occupations and Values*. Glencoe, Ill.: The Free Press, 1957.

Schwartz, Barry N. and Disch, Robert, eds. *White Racism*. New York: Dell Publishing Co.

Sherif, Muzafer and Cantril, Hadley. *The Psychology of Ego*. New York: John Wiley and Sons, 1947.

Simon, Herbert A. *Administrative Behavior*. New York: Free Press, 1966.

Skolnick, Jerome H., ed. *The Politics of Protest: A Task Report on the Cause and Prevention of Violence*. New York: Simon and Schuster, 1969.

Smith, Russell E., and Zietz, Dorothy. *American Social Welfare Institutions*. New York: John Wiley and Sons, Inc., 1970.

Stahl, O. Glenn. *Public Personnel Administration*. New York: Harper and Row, 1962.

Stein, Harold. *Public Administration and Policy Development: A Case Book*. New York: Harcourt, Brace and World, Inc., 1952.

Tappan, Frances M. *Toward Understanding Administration in the Medical Environment*. New York: Macmillan Co., 1968.

Terry, Robert W. *For Whites Only*. Grand Rapids: William B. Eerdmans Publishing Co., 1970.

Warren, Roland. "Types of Purposive Social Change at the Community Level." In *Readings in Community Organization Practice*, Kramer, Ralph M., and Specht, Harry, eds. Englewood Cliffs, N.J.: Prentice-Hall, Inc., 1969.

Wilcox, Preston. *White Is*. New York: Grove Press, Inc., 1970.

Wilensky, Harold L., and Lebeaux, Charles N. *Industrial Society and Social Welfare*. 2nd ed. New York: Free Press, 1965.

Woodson, Carter G. *The Negro Professional Man and the Community*. Washington, D.C.: Association for the Study of Negro Life and History, 1934.

Wright, Nathan. *Let's Face Racism*. New York: Thomas Nelson Publishers, 1971.

Periodicals

Bennett, Lerone, Jr. "Liberation." *Ebony*, Vol. XXV, (August 1970), 36-45.

Billingsley, Andrew. "Bureaucratic and Professional Orientation Patterns in Social Casework." *Social Service Review*, 4, (December 1964), 400-407.

Blake, J. Herman. "Black Nationalism." *The Annals*, 382, (March 1969), 24.

Boggs, James and Grace, L. "Uprooting Racism and Racists in the United States." *Negro Digest*, Vol. 19, (January 1970), 20-22.

Booker, Simeon. "Ticker Tape U.S.A." *Jet*, XL, (March 1971).

Boskin, Joseph and Rosenstone, Robert A. "Introduction." *The Annals*, Vol. 382, (March 1969), ix.

Butts, Hugh F. "White Racism: Its Origins, Institutions, and the Implications for Professional Practice in Mental Health." *International Journal of Psychiatry*, Vol. 8, No. 6, (December 1969), 914-44.

Clark, John Henry. "The Growth of Racism in the West." *Black World*, Vol. 19, (October 1970), 4-10.

Cohen, Robert H. "Welfare: Race and Reform." *Civil Rights Digest*, (Fall 1969), 20-25.

Comer, James P. "White Racism: Its Roots, Form and Function." *American Journal of Psychiatry*, Vol. 126, No. 6, (December 1969).

Cross, William J. "The Negro-to-Black Conversion Experience." *Black World*, Vol. XX, (July 1971), 13-27.

Delany, Lloyd T. "The White American Psyche—Exploration of Racism." *Freedom Ways*, Vol. 8, (Summer 1968).

Dumont, Matthew P. "The Changing Face of Professionalism." *Social Policy*, (May/June 1970), 26.

Epstein, Irwin. "Organizational Careers, Professionalism, and Social Workers Radicalism." *Social Service Review*, Vol. 44, (June 1970), 122-30.

Etzioni, Amitai. "Two Approaches to Organizational Analysis: A Critique and a Suggestion." *Administrative Science Quarterly*, (1960), 275-78.

Florey, John. "Chicanos and Coalitions as a Force for Change." *Social Casework*, LI, (May 1971), 269-73.

Francois, Terry A. "A Black Man Looks at Racism." *Reader's Digest*, (September 1969).

Friedman, Murray. "Is White Racism the Problem?" *Commentary*, (January 1969).

Gold, Steve. "Unlearning White Racism." *Liberation*, (March/April 1969), 21-29.

Gouldner, Alvin W. "Cosmopolitans and Locals: Toward an Analysis of Latent Social Roles." *Administrative Science Quarterly*, Vols. II and III, (December 1957 and 1958), 201-306.

Hamilton, Charles V. "Black Americans and the Modern Political Struggle." *Black World*, (May 1970), 5-9.

Henderson, Lenneal. "Engineers for Liberation." *Black Politician*, (April 1970).

Heppler, Arthur E. "The Game of Black and White at Hunter Point." *Transaction*, (April 1970).

Honey, John C. "Higher Education for Public Service." *Public Administration Review*, XXVII, (November 1967), 294-321.

Howie, Don. "The Origins of Racism." *Negro Digest*, (February 1970), 39-46.

Hughes, Everett. "Institutional Office and the Person." *American Journal of Sociology*, Vol. XLIII, (1943), 404-13.

Kaufman, Herbert. "The Next Step in Case Studies." *Public Administration Review*, Vol. 18, No. 4, (Winter 1958), 52-9.

Ladner, Joyce and Stafford, Walter. "Black Repression in the Cities: An Analysis of Institutional Racism in the 70's." *Black Scholar*, (April 1970).

Lewis, Harold. "Societal Crisis—Stratagem for Social Work Education." *Education for Social Work,* (Spring 1969).

Lewis, Sinclair O. "Racism in Counseling." *Counselor Education and Supervision,* (Fall 1969).

Miller, S. M., and Rein, Martin. "Participation, Poverty, and Administration." *Public Administration Review,* Vol. XXIX, No. 1, (January/February 1969), 15-25.

Moore, Howard, Jr. "Racism As Justice." *Rhythm,* (June 1970).

Page, Richard S. "A New Public Administration." *Public Administration Review,* Vol. XXIX, No. 3, (May/June 1969), 303.

"Political Science Association Offers Aid to Blacks." *Jet Magazine,* (January 30, 1971), 4.

"Protest in the Sixties." *The Annals,* Special Issue, (March 1969).

Rainwater, Lee. "Open Letter on White Justice and the Riots." *Transaction,* (September 1960), 63.

Rapport, Lydia. "In Defense of Social Work: An Examination of Stress in the Profession." *Social Service Review,* (March 1960), 63.

Rensenbrink, John. "America's Racial Crisis: The Advent of New Consciousness." *Current,* (November 1969), 17-22.

Sanders, Charles L. "Black Assertion Among Black Professionals." *Journal of National Medical Association,* (November 1971).

————. "The Growth of the Association of Black Social Workers." *Social Casework,* LI, (May 1970), 277-84.

Schuman, Howard. "Sociological Racism." *Transaction,* (December 1969), 44-8.

Shannon, Barbara E. "Implications of White Racism for Social Work Practice." *Social Casework,* (May 1970), 270-6.

Specht, Harry. "Disruptive Tactics." *Social Work,* Vol. 14, (April 1969), 5-15.

Smythe, Hugh H. "Changing Patterns in Negro Leadership." *Social Forces,* Vol. 29, No. 2, (December 1950).

Strom, Alfred M. "NASW Membership: Characteristics, Development and Salaries." *Personnel Information,* XII, National Association of Social Workers, (May 1969), 35.

Thomas, Charles W. "Boys No More: Some Social-Psychological Aspects of the New Black Ethnic." *American Behavioral Scientist,* (March/April 1969), 38-43.

White, Orion. "The Dialectical Organization: An Alternative to Bureaucracy." *Public Administration Review,* (January/February, 1969), 82.

Wilcox, Preston. "Social Policy and White Racism." *Social Policy,* (May/June, 1970), 41-46.

Newspapers

"National Association of Black Social Workers, Annual Conference, Chicago, Illinois." *Amsterdam News,* Vol. 61, No. 34, (August 21, 1971).
"Position Statement: Community Control and Decentralization." National Association of Black Social Workers, New York City Chapter. *Amsterdam News,* (November 25, 1968).
"Statement on Black Rebellion." *Amsterdam News,* (October 21, 1967).

Reports

American Council on Education. Report of the Commission for University Education. *University Education for Administration in Hospitals.* Washington, D.C., (1954).
National Advisory Commission on Civil Disorders. *Report of the National Advisory Commission on Civil Disorders.* New York: Bantam Books, 1968. 10.
Statistics on Social Work Education, 1970/71. New York: Council on Social Work Education, (1971).
Stevenson, Jerome C. *Some Observations on Attitudes of Blacks Toward United Way Organizations in Five Cities.* Community Fund of Chicago, Inc., July 1971.
"Toward a National Health Program." *National Urban League Position,* (February 1971).
U. S. Commission on Civil Rights. *Racism In America and How To Combat It.* Washington, D.C.: Government Printing Office, 1970.

Proceedings

American College of Hospital Administrators. *By-Laws Adopted at Annual Meeting on August 15, 1969.* Chicago: 1969.
Burgest, David R. "Social Work and White Racism." *Proceedings of 42nd Annual Meeting of Georgia Conference on Social Welfare.* Atlanta, Ga.: 1969.

National Conference of Black Social Workers, Philadelphia, Pa. *The Black Family.* February 21-23, 1969.

National Conference on Social Welfare. *The Social Welfare Forum — 1970 Proceedings.* New York: Columbia University Press, 1970.

Unpublished Materials

American Hospital Association. "Statement on Health Care for the Disadvantaged." Approved by House of Delegates, February, 1970.

American Political Science Association. "Position Paper: Black Caucus." September, 1969.

Atlanta University, Department of Political Science. "Newsletter, NCBPS." Atlanta, Ga.: September 1971.

Baker, Houston, Director, Freedmen's Medical Center, Washington, D.C. "Private Files: Notes on the National Conference of Hospital Administrators." (Undated).

Detore, Robert R. "Recommendations for the National Work Study Recruitment Program in Hospital Administration for Minority Group Members." Association of University Programs in Hospital Administration, Washington, D.C. (1971) Mimeographed.

First Annual National Conference of Black Political Scientists. (Brochure) Atlanta, Ga.: May 1970.

Frederickson, H. George. "Organization Theory and the New Public Adminstration." Unpublished paper. Maxwell School of Public Affairs, Syracuse University, 1969.

Havrileshy, Catherine, and Wilcox, Preston. *A Selected Bibligraphy on White Institutional Racism.* Unpublished. New York: Afram Associates, Inc., 1969.

Hershey, Gary. "Emergent Militant Professionalism in the Urban Public Service: A Framework for Analysis." Unpublished paper. New York University Graduate School of Public Administration, January, 1970.

Mann, Joseph A. President-Elect, National Association of Health Service Executives. Speech delivered in Brooklyn, N.Y., July 7, 1970.

National Association of Black Social Workers. "Position Statement: National Conference on Social Welfare, New York." May 20, 1969.

National Association of Health Service Executives. "Brochure for Membership." National Headquarters, Baltimore, Md. 1971.

National Association of Health Service Executives. "Constitution and By-Laws." National Headquarters, Baltimore, Md. September 1970 (revised).

National Association of Health Service Executives: "Meeting Agendas: Houston, Texas, September 1970 and Chicago, Illinois, February, 1971." "Minutes of Meeting Held at Provident Hospital, Baltimore, Md., June 12, 1971."

National Association of Health Service Executives. "Position Paper: Health and the Black Condition." National Headquarters, Baltimore, Md.

National Association of Health Service Executives. "Program for Strengthened Graduate Programs in Business for Blacks with Interest in the Non-Profit Sector." Education Committee. Baltimore, Md., February 1971.

National Association of Health Service Executives. "Position Paper: Submitted to New York City Health and Hospital Corporation." New York City Chapter, August 1971.

Ramsay, Annette. *Understanding White Racist Thought: A Bibliography*. Unpublished. New York: Afram Associates, Inc., May 1970.

Rice, Haynes. *Proposed Budget for National Association of Health Service Executives*. 1971.

Rice, Haynes. "Proposed Summer Recruitment Plan." National Association of Health Service Executives, Education Committee, Baltimore, Md., May 1971. (Mimeographed)

Standback, Howard. "Proposal: National Institute of Black Social Thought." National Association of Black Social Workers, July 1971. (Mimeographed)

Student Affiliates of the National Association of Health Service Executives. "Position Statement." Chicago, Ill., February 1971. (Mimeographed)

White, Henry J. *Roster of the NAHSE and Member Status in American College of Hospital Administration*. July 1970. (Mimeographed)

Williams, Cenie J., National President, National Association of Black Social Workers. "Speech Delivered at National Conference of Black Social Workers, Chicago, Ill., April 4, 1971."